Best Wishes

Frederick Bailes

Hidden Power

for

Human Problems

$\backsim$ $\backsim$ $\backsim$

Man is a stream whose source is hidden.
Our being is descending into us from
we know not whence . . . We lie in the lap
of immense Intelligence, which makes us
receivers of its truth and organs of
its activity . . . we do nothing of ourselves
but allow a passage to its beams.

Prayer is the contemplation of the facts
of life from the highest point of view . . .
it is the spirit of God pronouncing
his works good . . . for the Maker of
all things and all persons stands
behind us, and casts his dread
omniscience *through* us *over* things.

Ralph Waldo Emerson

$\backsim$ $\backsim$ $\backsim$

HIDDEN POWER
for
HUMAN PROBLEMS

by

Frederick Bailes

SECOND EDITION

PRENTICE-HALL, INC.
ENGLEWOOD CLIFFS, N. J.

© 1957 by
FREDERICK BAILES

LIBRARY OF CONGRESS CATALOG CARD NUMBER: 57-13274

First printing .... October, 1957
Second printing ...... January, 1958
Third printing .... May, 1958
Fourth printing ...... August, 1958
Fifth printing .... March, 1959

PRINTED IN THE UNITED STATES OF AMERICA
38695

To Mati

Table of Contents

One loss accepted brings others
Blessings counted multiply
Every ending is a beginning

Part 2: How to Use the Creative Process: Methods, Techniques and Sample Treatments

A "fog" prayer treatment

The "invisible-wave" treatment

The "invisible-wave" method in obscure cases

The "contracting-expanding" method

The importance of spiritual awareness

The power of the quiet mind

The "authoritative" method

Nothing comes without our consent

The "convergent" method

"How much can happen through me?"

The healing law is the law of love

Anyone can cultivate love

> Some people dominate life.
> Others let life
> dominate them.
> What makes the difference?

• *Victory and defeat are all around you*

Read your daily newspapers, listen to the talk of your neighbors, keep your eyes open on the streets. What do you see and hear?

People come in all shapes, sizes and peculiarities but over and above all you see the one great difference. Some of them are happy and successful and some of them are not.

Some stride confidently from day to day, piling success upon success and one happy moment upon another. They seem to be endowed with some *special force*. While others drag themselves through each twenty-four hours as if life itself were a burden and *more* troubles were tomorrow's only expectation.

- *Are you a strider or a limper?*

In which category have you been living? Or do you belong to a third classification of people who *limp* through life: they're never completely miserable but they're never really happy; they're never complete failures but success is always just beyond their reach; they're never sick enough to go to the hospital but some little illness is always chipping away their health.

- *How much longer will you ignore the law that makes this startling difference among people?*

You need no words of mine to convince you that this difference does exist among human beings. But if you have been one of the unhappy ones here is an *unquestionable fact:* you have *not* been making use of the LAW that makes the difference. For it is the use of this great Law, whether it is a conscious or unconscious use, that brings to the world all the health, prosperity, and peace of mind that it has.

A new Law? Of course not; only *newly-discovered!*

Within the past half-century more has been

discovered about the laws that shape human life than was known in all the centuries before.

- ## *This book explains the creative law and supplies methods for putting it into operation*

There is a creative law older than man, operating ceaselessly in him. It can furnish the dynamic needed to enable him to reach those goals he has selected.

It operates inflexibly and without deviation. It is always creating *something*, with or without man's consent. It creates bad things and it creates good things; happiness and unhappiness, success and failure.

But—and here is the actual key to living— man can set the direction of its activity by cooperating with it. Let me say that again in another way: *man can direct this law for his own betterment*. The law *exists* to serve him. And it is as certain, orderly, and unchangeable as are the laws of science.

To make that law and the understanding of it available to a greater number of people I have written this book. To make it as easy as possible for you to start deriving the benefits of this law I have included specific details on methods and techniques.

● *This message has been tested and proved over and over again*

I have taught this message for over *thirty years*, here and abroad. Even when presented through interpreters in foreign countries it has demonstrated its power.

Every Sunday, rain or shine, for several years, the congregations that have come to hear me tell of this great law have outgrown auditorium after auditorium. Today almost twenty-five hundred men and women pack one of the largest halls in the West to hear it every week. Why this great interest? *Because these people have found that it works! That the message is true!*

● *What the creative law has done for others*

These men and women crowd that theater because of one thing alone—they hear something which enables them to get results.

They have found: Healing for apparently incurable illness,
Advancement in business
where before they had
been stymied,
Peace of mind where there
had been turmoil,
Harmony in their immedi-
ate environment where
there had been discord.

Families have been reunited, unmanageable
children have been straightened out, alcoholics
have been freed of their destructive habits, lonely
men and women have drawn love and marriage
into their lives.

● *This law operates in every level of society*

The people who have used and benefited from
this law, to my own personal knowledge, come
from every area of society and income bracket.
They are heads of corporations, and the men who
drive their trucks, motion picture stars and stage
hands, university professors and their students,
housewives, stenographers, professional men, and
carpenters.

These people are characterized by a singular *decisiveness* of character. They have found something which has taken the guesswork out of their strivings. They have learned to practice the law by which things are brought to pass.

● *Any law is your master until you understand it*

As soon as a law is understood it becomes your servant. But you cannot master a law just by hearing what it will do. You must trace its complications. Study it. Put it to the test by practicing it.

And you must be absolutely honest with yourself. Never avoiding the truth or excusing yourself. Never run away from the disclosure of hidden, unworthy motives. Never shrink from the necessary steps to be taken in the conquest of your lesser self.

You must remake yourself, clear to your very center. This means careful reading, observation, and sincere effort.

To help you in this study, I have placed at the end of each chapter, in rather large type, a thought-provoking lesson or statement. I recommend that you clip these pages from the book as you finish each chapter and put them in places where you will see them often. You might place them beside the bathroom mirror, the bedroom mirror, or near the doorways for instance. (The pages are not numbered so that when you take them out it won't interfere with the numbering of the book.)

- ### There is nothing "tricky" about the creative law

This book is not concerned with passing psychological tricks, because there is nothing tricky about the law in question.

In the following pages you will learn the exact nature of this law, but I might state it briefly here. This law says that *all thoughts become reality*. When we let the Infinite Intelligence—or God—think His thoughts through our minds *the law will then be turning perfect thoughts into perfect experience.*

- ### The power to make you do what you want to do

A judge of the California courts said to me once: "I know that I must change my inner thought patterns. I want to and intend to do so." Then he asked, almost desperately: "But just how do I go about it? I have tried and can't do it! My mind seems to agree to my desire, and then it goes on just as it has always done. I am left more baffled and frustrated than before because I have seen new light but find myself unable to live up to it."

Like so many people, this man had found an *ethic*, that is, a set of principles by which to live. What he needed was a *dynamic*; the power to make him do what he wanted to do.

• *This book has been planned to make the process crystal clear*

I have written this book in two Parts.

The first will tell you how, over thirty years ago, I rediscovered this Creative Law (it actually saved my life), how the teaching of it developed to the point where today hundreds of thousands of people live by it. The first Part will explain the Law so that there will be no doubt about your understanding it, and it will show the Law at work in the lives of various people who have come to me for help. (You will learn a great lesson from the businessman who came to me, angry and red of face, to tell me that I had taught erroneously over the radio. His familiar habit of watching the sun set over the ocean became the beginning of his return to serenity through the Creative Process.)

- *Part Two will supply you with all the
  necessary methods for using
  the Creative Process*

In Part Two there are four sections. These can be the beginning of a new life for you.

There is a complete discussion on *how to give a healing prayer treatment*. In this section you will learn *why* you must accept the possibility of success before you start, and *why* you do not pray against any specific disease or physical condition.

It answers such questions as:

- How long should a prayer treatment be?

- How often should prayer treatment be given?

- How is prayer treatment affected by my personal "unworthiness?"

- Can the law of the Creative Process be used at the same time that a person is being treated by a doctor of medicine?

Everything necessary for your immediate use of the powerful forces of the Creative Law is here made clear and workable.

● *There are definite techniques to help set the process in motion*

In another section of Part Two you are given the complete details of five different methods for setting the actual Creative Process in motion. They are methods I have worked out for myself over the past thirty years; methods that I use today in treating the people who come to me for help.

These methods are not magic wands that produce results with a vague wave of the hand. They have been formulated from an observance of human nature itself.

People think in *pictures*. Words are the tools that help us communicate these pictures to others. *These methods actually allow you to picture the Creative Process at work.*

Thus your own belief and efforts are made more powerful and so more effective.

I have called these methods by the following names:

- 1. The Fog Method
- 2. The Invisible Wave Method
- 3. The Contracting-expanding Method
- 4. The Authoritative Method
- 5. The Convergent Method

- *There is a blueprint of parent thoughts,
  master thoughts for overcoming each of
  them, and a condensed prayer treatment
  for each of the categories*

Although a whole book could be written
on the various troubles growing out of parent
thoughts, in a special section I have given enough
to enable you to identify any condition that may
be troubling you. Accompanying each is the master thought you must use to counteract the parent
thought.

Finally, this section supplies you with condensed prayer treatments to be used in each circumstance. These prayer treatments are just long
enough to include all the necessary elements. But
you can add your own thoughts and words so that
something of *your own consciousness* is in the
treatment.

To make this addition of your own thoughts
and words easier, after each of my printed prayer
treatments I have had blank lines added so that you
may put down your own words. Then you won't
forget them and you'll have the whole prayer in
one place.

● *You can choose to start a new life*

People are funny. Tell them that it is possible for them to throw off the burden of aimless, empty, troublesome living that has been weighing down their previous years. They'll look at you interestedly, even nod their heads in agreement. But in their hearts what are they saying? "It's too good to be true!"

If that little phrase of doubt is crawling around in your heart, *pluck it out!*

Nothing is surer than this: if you want to change your life, to live the happy, successful existence you were meant to have, *it is within your grasp.*

The principle of beginning again is so simple it's almost startling. A new life is yours if you choose to take it.

● *Would you give seven days to an effort to remake your life?*

Sometimes, to people who understand Creative Law and are using it to build a new life, the change is almost immediate. To others it comes slowly, because they have so much to overcome, or they are not conscientiously applying the principles they have learned.

But with complete faith, I can make this statement:

IF YOU PRACTICE THE PRINCIPLES OF THE CREATIVE PROCESS AS SET FORTH IN THE FOLLOWING PAGES YOU WILL SEE AND FEEL A NEW FORCE IN YOUR LIFE WITHIN SEVEN DAYS.

The experience of thirty years, and the observance of thousands of people, backs up the truth of that statement.

- *It's what you do that counts—not how you feel*

One of the strangest facts about this Creative Law is that it will work for you whether you believe it wholeheartedly or not. THE LAW DOES NOT DEPEND ON YOUR BELIEF. IT IS TRUE IN ITSELF.

Your "faith" in this Law need only extend as far as the effort to put it in motion. After that, the Law moves under its own volition.

You can even put this thought into your prayer treatment. Say: "The Law is working for me—as it works for everyone—whether or not I feel that it is true."

● *If you have read this far—you have made a beginning*

What made you pick up this book? Was it idle curiosity, or was it a genuine interest in learning the laws by which your life can be made better? Did you come across it by accident in a friend's house, a library, a bookstore?

Or was it something more than accident, something more than interest or curiosity?

Was it the Creative Process itself that led you to this book, and urged you to read this far? From what is known of this Law, such a thing is very possible. *Some* unconscious knowledge of the Creative Law burns in everyone's heart like a small flame.

Read on, and that small flame will grow brighter and stronger until, in the full and practiced use of the Creative Process, dark attitudes will be consumed and from the ashes of the old life a new, substantial, and more wonderful life shall have arisen.

● *To get everything possible out of this book
at your first reading give yourself the
following prayer treatment before
you begin*

Even as you read these words, your mind is
probably troubled by something. In such a frame
of mind you may miss many of the points and
might not come to a full appreciation of the Creative Law.

To relax yourself and get into the best frame
of mind give yourself the following prayer treatment.

Think of the most peaceful scene you can remember. Let your mind's eye rove over the scene
as you recall the things that made it peaceful, or
beautiful or memorable.

When your mind has become permeated with
the colorful serenity of the scene, read the following words. Read a phrase at a time and think about
each phrase. Let the thoughts sink into your consciousness.

> I am made in the image of God. Therefore,
> the peace that is God's nature must likewise be
> at the heart and center of my being.

Nothing was ever intended to interfere with this peace. Whatever is at the bottom of my distress has no place in the Infinite Plan.

I let myself sink into the arms of the Eternal like a tired child in its mother's arms. Peace steals over me and the quiet of the Eternal wraps itself around me.

Be still, soul, and know that I am God. Father, I become still in Thy presence. I feel now the Infinite stillness. Even though the storm rages without, I feel Thy peace within. I am quiet, relaxed, passive in Thy unruffled peace.

PART ONE

THE CREATIVE PROCESS:

Discovery, Development, and Explanation

chapter one

The "Incurable"

Finds a Cure

IN THE AUTUMN OF 1915 A YOUNG MAN WAS DYING. FEW would have guessed it, passing him as he walked the streets of London. The only obvious symptoms were his unusual pallor and the sugary sweetness of his breath.

Competent medical authorities had informed this young fellow that he had diabetes, a supposedly incurable malady; on a careful diet, they advised, he might live eighteen months. (At that time Dr. Banting had not yet given insulin to the world.)

The young man was miserably confused. How could this be? Why had God allowed such a destructive disease to fall upon him, whose important years had been devoted to getting ready for God's service? He had thought God would be on *his* side, for he was a medical missionary student.

Hard work, cheap meals, persistent study into the small hours of the morning he had cheerfully accepted. With high expectancy, he had looked forward to what he would eventually accomplish for his fellow men.

He was not just a dedicated grind. The tides of life had always run strong and full in him. He was an athlete, like most of his fellow New Zealanders. Golf, swimming, tennis, cricket, football, bicycle-racing, weight-lifting, boxing, wrestling, hunting, and fishing were part of him. He loved life; he wanted desperately to live.

And now, in one stroke, it was all to be taken away. He could not believe it. He *would* not believe it.

One day, a few weeks after he had received his death sentence, he idly picked up a book in a friend's house. That simple action changed the course of his life—for the knowledge he gained from the book not only cured his supposedly fatal illness, but started him on a missionary venture totally different from the one he had planned.

The author of the book, Thomas Troward, was an Englishman, a devout churchman, who had served as a judge in India. He had studied the Indian religions, Christianity, and Judaism.

In his book he did not stress physical healing particularly, but he outlined a deep-lying principle, flowing throughout the universe, that takes men's desires, hopes, and choices, and condenses them into form. He showed that this is being done every time that we think. With judicial logic he built up a case to prove his assertion that any of us can bring into his life anything that he wishes, through the Infinite Creative Process operating through the mind of the individual.

2

The Creative Process Saves a Life

The young diabetic belonged to one of the most orthodox branches of the church. At first he shrank from some of Troward's unorthodox statements. But what did he have to lose? Troward's Biblical interpretations might be correct—so he decided he would give his idea a fair trial.

If the young man had not succeeded in his venture, you would not be reading this book—for I was that young man.

My recovery from diabetes was not something I imagined. I had occasion to see it put to exhaustive medical tests when I later applied for life insurance. The company would have refused me when I reported my medical history if I had not insisted I was now completely free of the disease, volunteering to undergo examination by experts. Under constant supervision I was fed considerable amounts of sugar, and tests were made for its presence in the proper places in my body. The doctors declared me a Class A risk and the company issued the policy.

Since then I have proved that this universal principle can be applied to any situation. It is by no means confined to the healing of the body. The same law that restored my health works in the business world. It is the same principle by which food, securities, automobiles, or real estate are successfully sold. It can draw love into a person's life, enable him to pass difficult examinations, bring harmony into chaotic surroundings. It is the one universal principle by which one can bring into his life anything he desires without hurting other persons.

3

My first experience of the unlimited usefulness of this law was in 1921, when I went to work for the public utility that served the city of Beloit. Five experienced company employees and I were given the task of selling a half million dollars' worth of preferred stock to the customers of the company. I was totally inexperienced, but my use of this principle enabled me to far outsell the other five. Later I used the same principle in selling millions of dollars' worth of high-grade bonds in Illinois and Wisconsin, against stiff competition. This was certainly not due to any brilliance in me, for most of my competitors were brighter.

The law—which I call *Creative Law*—will prove itself in any human activity in which we use and trust it.

The Law by Which the Creative Process Works

A simple statement of Creative Law would be that man lives in a surrounding River of Mind, into which his thoughts fall, and which ceaselessly turns *all* these thoughts into form. The River seems to obey man, because Its nature is to translate his thoughts into experience. Its power is limitless; Its knowledge of ways and means is infinite; Its willingness to produce is without the slightest reservation. It is the working side of the Eternal God.

Now, if all of a man's thoughts are turned into experiences, into events in his life, it follows that if he wants perfect experience, he must think perfect thoughts. We might despair at this point. But here is the key and the promise of a life fulfilled beyond anyone's imaginings. We do not have to grub up perfect thoughts from our pathetically imperfect minds and imaginations. The Infinite Creator is already thinking the thoughts that will bring us what we want. We need only *choose* to *let God think these thoughts through us*. The impersonal obedient Servant, the River, the Creative Law will do the rest.

What Do the Scientists Think?

It will be remembered that Roger Babson asked Charles Steinmetz, the Wizard of Schenectady, which line of research would show the greatest development during the next fifty years. Instead of discussing the electrical field as might have been expected, Steinmetz said he believed the greatest discoveries would be made along the line of *spiritual* force.

"Here is a force," he is reported to have said, "which history proves to have been the greatest power in the development of men. Yet we have only been playing with it. We have never seriously studied it as we have the material forces. Some day, people will learn that material things do not bring happiness and are of little use in making men creative and personally powerful. In the near future, the scientists will turn their laboratories over to the study of God and prayer and the spiritual forces which as yet have scarcely been touched. *When this day comes, the world will see more advancement in one generation than it has seen in the past four*." Steinmetz might have said "the past forty thousand years" and been correct.

Carl Jung recognized this spiritual element when he said that in his patients over thirty-five years of age the physical problem was at base a spiritual problem, and that only those were cured who re-established their contact with God. Thus, the method recommended in this book goes beyond psychosomatic medicine; perhaps it would be more correct to say that the psychosomatic concept stops short of the spiritual dynamic necessary to make it a complete system.

Christ Spoke of this Law

Two thousand years ago Jesus tried to show that one cannot bang on the gates of heaven and get a divine hand-out. He emphasized that he came to fulfill "the law." He tried to teach men that they were made in the image and likeness of God. He saw them held in the chains of their false beliefs, believing themselves to be miserable, ill, poor, wicked, under God's displeasure. He pitied their ignorance of their true state. He knew that their misery and unhappiness were the results of their wrong views of themselves and he said, "It is done unto you as you believe."

We are never punished *for* our sins, but by them. All "sins" ultimately are the holding of wrong thoughts. "The wages of sin is death" is not the dictum of an offended judge; it is an unemotional statement of cause and effect, similar to "The result of reckless driving will be an accident."

"How Do I Go about It?"

Earlier I referred to the fact that a judge had said to me recently, "I know that I must alter my inner thought patterns. I want to and intend to do so. But just *how* do I go about it? My reach exceeds my grasp. My mind is intractable. It nods assent to my desire, then goes on just as it has always done. I am left more baffled and frustrated

6

than before because I have seen new light but find myself unable to live up to it."

That was the problem I faced when I had diabetes.

To begin with I had Troward's astonishing concept which I put this way: God is obedient to man as man becomes obedient to God. Man needs God for power; God needs man as an outlet.

Next, I had to learn to give my directions to the "Servant." For God's Creative Law is a general law that I wanted to specialize for my own development. Not by altering the law or causing it to deviate; that would be impossible anyway. But by providing a set of conditions that were not explicitly provided for in the law.

For example, there is a general law of electricity, yet the Infinite never created a vacuum sweeper. But someone, discovering the law of electricity, provided it with a set of conditions that made it sweep floors. Another made it toast bread; still another, to run an elevator or to send a broadcast out over the airwaves. It is the selfsame law but adapted to meet the individual conditions desired.

I wished to provide the conditions through which God's creativity would restore my pancreas (the organ that in diabetes does not function properly) and my whole body to perfect health.

Thought Patterns Must Be Corrected

Starting with the assumption of the Mind of God, Whose perfect thoughts are perfectly carried out by the Servant, it was apparent that my thinking diverged from the perfect thinking of the Infinite—otherwise I would

7

be in perfect health. My imperfect images were constantly being wrought into form along with His perfect thought patterns. The result was a mixed manifestation, much of which was bad, some of which was good. The more successful I was in correcting my dominant thought patterns, the more singleness would be brought into my affairs. "If thine eye (thy vision) be *single*, thy whole body shall be full of light."

We Learn by Practice, Not by Theory

I would like to emphasize at this point that seven days of practicing what I am about to explain will produce more proof than volumes of theoretical explanations. "This is the way; walk ye in it." Throughout the ages millions have looked at it, examined it, dissected it, pondered it, discussed it, criticized it, even sighed for it. But these theorists have not been healed. Only those who have actually walked in it received their healing. Joshua told the Israelites that every piece of ground that they set their foot on would be theirs. They would never gain the Promised Land by sitting on Mt. Pisgah and feasting their eyes on it. It was necessary that they actually set foot on it. They had to launch themselves on a definite campaign, do something practical actually to possess it.

The Three Steps

In directing the Creative Process into action for us, we must take three simple steps.

First, we must *Understand Creative Law*. We must know how It works and we must know how our own acts fit into Its workings. This understanding is necessary in directing the Creative Process in the same way, say, that understanding of a gearshift is necessary in driving a standard model car. Certain saintly people seem to come equipped with automatic transmissions that set the Infinite in motion for them without their conscious thought. But the rest of us must consciously go through the separate operations, understanding each one.

After we understand that the Law turns our thoughts into form, the second step is to furnish it with the correct thought to work with. Most of our thoughts are pictures, or images, so a simple statement of the second step is that we must *form the correct image.*

And in the third step we *release the image to the "Servant," Creative Law.*

I shall explain how I took each of the three steps in finding a cure for my diabetes. Definite improvement began to show within a few weeks after I started to use this new approach to my illness, but it was going to be a few years before I was completely healed.

1. *Understand Creative Law.* During the years it took me to learn just what the correct method was, I was often discouraged and tempted to place the cause of my misery *outside* of myself—in God, or in a body operating by laws not under God's or my control. It is a temptation that comes to most of us.

But each of us stands today exactly where he belongs by the right of consciousness. Some persons cringe at such a statement, shrink from it, adduce arguments and apparent proof to show that their sufferings are the faults of others, or at least not their own. Such persons are the only incurables in the world. They will never be able to move

9

from their present misery as long as they cling to this false belief, for it is a fundamental that each man is the maker of his own heaven or hell.

Sometimes I would complain that I had done everything I could—that if God had loved me He would have healed me long since.

The fact of the matter is that God operates always through His Law side as well as His Love side. The Law side will *always* produce the same kind of results when properly applied. Two students take up flying; after a given number of hours of study each is allowed to solo. One flies beautifully; the other crashes. God's whim does not enter in here. One student has come to grasp the principles of flight; the other has left a gap somewhere in his mastery of the laws of aerodynamics. There was a similar reason for my failure or success in healing.

He who approaches the Creative Law of his own thought correctly will find that it *always* responds to him. There is no mystery about it. But this law is completely impersonal. It is not affected by our great need, our promises of reformation, or our pleading. It responds to one thing alone, our compliance with its principles. It never fails when we approach it intelligently.

2. *Form the Correct Image.* The view that I stood alone, that everything depended upon my own *unaided* struggle, would have been a major barrier to the constructive working of the Creative Law for good. This one false belief could have barred the complete manifestation in me of the perfect images held in the Mind of the Infinite.

Therefore, when I composed myself to join with God

in giving directions to our Servant, I would first quietly declare something like this:

"I let my thought move out to the vastness of space, as though there were no such thing as a pancreas. With that I have nothing to do. I consider the heavens, the ceaseless movement of those tremendously heavy bodies which are being drawn through space with sublime ease. I think of the resistless flow of spiritual currents that are at this moment guiding, directing, controlling all of the mighty substance of the universe. I lose myself in a sense of the vastness of that force."

Here I had a new concept of the resistless Power of the Infinite—and a new appreciation of the willingness of the Almighty to intervene on my side. Surely, I thought, a God Who was willing to exert force to hurl giant unthinking masses of molten metal through space at unbelievable speeds must be willing to exert His force to reproduce Himself in sentient man, His own offspring!

In my directions to the Servant, after I had affirmed the Servant's inexorable power, I affirmed that God was thinking through me the perfect thoughts upon which the Servant would act, somewhat like this:

"No longer do I let my thoughts hover around a pancreas as a *physical* organ. I think of each organ as an idea of the Infinite, conceived before I was conceived. It is one separate and distinct idea of God. All of God's ideas are perfect. I refuse to think of it as having blot, blemish, or inaction. I see it as the willing servant of me the thinker, and this, my thought, is now being taken up by the Universal Thinker and brought forth into actuality. Not being an organ but an idea, it is a perfect idea now. I do not care what the laboratory shows; I now take God's view and see all of his ideas as being perfect. And it *is* so."

Notice that I *declared* the truth. I did not beg, plead, or request, for these approaches embody a doubt—a possibility of refusal. There is no room for doubt in directing the Creative Law. Though you may *feel* doubt, you do not act on it. Creative Law works not by your feelings, but by the images we *choose to form* and give to it to work with. This may seem ridiculously simple; all things are simple once we understand them.

3. *Release the Image to the Servant.* When, elaborating on the basic ideas, I had through the use of words affirmed what I call a *master thought*, I *released* this image to the Servant. My duty then was to go about my affairs, leaving the Servant to work undisturbed. When any doubt tried to intrude, I affirmed, "I'm glad it's in God's hands. I'm glad God is taking care of it."

The results at first were not striking. After some weeks, however, laboratory analysis showed that the pancreas was beginning to awake from its lethargy.

The course of improvement from then on, though quite irregular, was definite. Some weeks there would be a decided drop in the sugar index; other weeks would show a rise. But the high point of the sugar rise was never quite so high as the high point of the previous rise.

Here I had the first and the only worthwhile evidence that the idea of Creative Law was a sound one: it was working. To all theoretical objections my response is, "The proof of the pudding is in the eating. Try it; it works."

Persistence Pays Off—Diabetes Healed

The rest of my little epic is a simple story. I was better, but six years had passed, and I was not yet completely well. To put it another way, I was on the track, but not quite straight on. I seemed somehow to hold some hidden reservation. Somewhere in my prayers, in my directions to the Servant, there was some imperfection of which I was not fully aware.

Driven by the necessity to be rid of my terrible disease, I persisted in groping to find the *master thought* that would overcome the imperfect thought in me, doing away with the interference to God's restoration of my health. During this time I came to the United States, to Beloit, Wisconsin. In Beloit the laboratory reports at last reached the point where there was only "Sugar, a trace."

One evening I sat with elbows on desk, head on hands, eyes closed. Then I started, quietly and confidently, to declare something like this:

"Whatever is blocking my complete recovery must be some hidden strand of thought that holds some mental reservation. I am not aware of its nature, where it started, or what keeps it active. But it must be mine, whether I can trace my way to it or not.

"I do not want it to keep operating, therefore I now declare that it is a vestige of my former destructive thought. I emphatically state that it is completely out of line with the Infinite Thinker's thoughts which are trying to manifest perfectly through me. It is a squatter living on territory where it has no rights of any sort. I call in the law to evict, dissolve, and negate it *right now.*

13

"I wash my hands of it. I do not have to fight it, worry about it, or pay any attention to it. It is nothing trying to be something. It is no more real than the bogey man that scared me as a boy. I turn every last thread of my thought to the contemplation of that steady movement of the thought of God in me and through every single cell of my body.

"I think of Its beauty, Its unutterable harmonies, Its total unawareness of any resisting force, Its breathing of 'It is good' as It contemplates the universe It has brought into being. Quietly now I let myself drift into the innermost parts of that Infinite Mind, catch something of its unshakeable peace, knowing that this Mind flows through me as my mind."

I went on affirming the power of the Infinite and Its perfect image of my body, concluding by expressing my gratitude for the healing that I declared was taking place. My last words were the customary ones, "It *is* so."

I got up, went out, and walked along the bank of the Rock River in Wisconsin. I looked at the stars, trees, and river; quietly I said, "They are good, all good; for they too are ideas held by God."

The next laboratory report said, "Sugar negative."

It was so. It has never returned.

THE CREATIVE PROCESS

- When you allow the omnipotent God to think His creative thoughts through you, you are using the Creative Process.
- Since God can think only perfect thoughts, the more you surrender yourself to the Process the more perfect will your life become.

THE THREE STEPS OF THE CREATIVE PROCESS

1. *UNDERSTAND CREATIVE LAW*

   Understanding comes before use. Learn well the lessons in this book.

2. *FORM THE CORRECT IMAGE*

   Most people think in terms of pictures. You must form in your mind the image of the thing you desire so that the Creative Process can transform it into reality.

3. *RELEASE THE IMAGE TO THE SERVANT*

   Consciously dismiss the image from your mind, affirming at the same time: It's in God's hands. I'm glad God is taking care of it.

chapter two

Overcoming an Ulcer

MR. BLUDGIN WAS ANGRY! HE SAT FACING ME AND SAID, "I've just come from my doctor. He says I have a gastric ulcer. I've heard you say on the air that illness stems from the thought life, and that our fear of conditions brings them to pass. Well sir, how do you account for this? I've never feared an ulcer, never expected it, never imagined myself having it. But I have an ulcer just the same."

I knew him by reputation. He was a hard-hitting, successful businessman, a quick thinker who made decisions rapidly, was very sure of himself, impatient with wobbly-minded people. But now he needed help.

My reply was something like this: "Mr. Bludgin, your argument sounds plausible to you, but it can be answered. In the first place, I would never say that one gets an ulcer or any other condition by consciously thinking of *it*. The interaction of mind and body is more subtle and complicated. Many persons suffer from conditions they had never expected nor feared. Yet their thinking drew these conditions as surely as if they had sat down and written an order for them."

I pointed out to Mr. Bludgin that man is not always aware of the quality of his beliefs. Millions of persons delude themselves into thinking that they believe certain things, when examination proves that their *dominant* belief is something entirely opposite. To illustrate this I cited Henry Ford's famous Peace Ship in World War I.

Mr. Ford gathered a group of people who "believed in peace." They sailed for Europe to stop that war. Doubtless they all thought that they believed in peace. Yet subsequent events showed that they only "wanted" peace; their deeper, more fundamental belief was not in peace but in strife. For the ship was not long at sea when they began to quarrel among themselves.

Unquestionably they believed in trying to stop that particular war, but that was only a fraction of their belief. Each might have had a sincere yet selfish reason for wanting the war stopped. One might not have liked to see the waste of good materials; one might have had a son who might be drafted; one might have desired the re-establishment of trade relations with the Central Powers; one might have been inspired by the thought that his name would go down in history as one who helped stop the war; another might have gone along for the ride.

The human mind is slippery and evasive. It is easy to persuade oneself of belief in a certain thing, but since it is a law of mind that we eventually manifest only that in which we deeply believe, it is evident that this shipload of people were believers in peace only in a secondary way; otherwise their mission would have been completed in harmony. The fact that they parted in anger indicated that their major belief was in strife and cross-purposes.

The Great Teacher said, "The prince of this world cometh and hath (or findeth) nothing in me." By this He meant there was nothing in him that could possibly respond to the enticements or attacks of the prince of this world. Jesus believed first and utterly in the Father—and His actions showed it.

Mahatma Gandhi was the object of much derision but it never really touched him. His belief in peaceful non-violent resistance went deep. It applied not only to national affairs but to his entire personal life. He lived in a detached calm that was the wonder and the envy of those who contacted him.

Even the assassin's bullet could not cause Gandhi to hate. Like Socrates and Jesus, he never allowed the bitterness of his enemies to enter his soul. It rolled off these men because they never harbored hidden bitterness themselves. These men had a total belief in peace. The Ford party had only a restricted belief.

The fact that Gandhi, Socrates, and Jesus died at the hands of others does not invalidate this thesis. None of them feared death nor thought it the supreme tragedy.

Our Beliefs Cause Our Experiences

Mr. Bludgin had fallen into a quite understandable error. He had failed to trace the sequence of cause and effect in his thinking.

A person sees certain effects appearing in his world of affairs. He can see no corresponding cause. Soon he assumes that he is ill beset by fortune, fate, or God.

He asks, "I am a fairly decent person. Why should this come upon me?" He proceeds by easy stages to bewilderment, hurt, resentment, and a sense of the unfairness of things.

For more than a quarter of a century I have faced desperate men and women across my desk seeking my assistance. I came to understand that problems of body and circumstances are traceable to less than a dozen basic states of mind. These grow out of beliefs about life which are fundamentally false, but which are believed to be true.

Eventually I evolved a method of prayer treatment which has proved itself by its excellent results. The literature of psychosomatic medicine which has flowered since then seems to approach man's ills from a similar point of view, in that the patient's basic beliefs about life determine his illness or health. I have given the name *parent thoughts* to the false beliefs, and *master thoughts* to their corrective opposites.

Theory of Parent Thoughts

Throughout the ages mankind has developed a number of basic beliefs about life. They are in the nature of general beliefs widely held by the race. Repeated in succeeding generations until they have gradually become imbedded in the race thought, they have become part of the warp and woof of human thinking.

The human race has had much experience of sorrow, hurt, trickery, defeat. It has also had many experiences of victory and happiness, but the preponderance of experience has been negative. Therefore, although the child is not born into the world fear-ridden, he carries in the lower depths of his mind the *unconscious racial memory* of all the buried experiences of his antecedents. These form the fertile soil in which his own personal experiences are to take root.

These half-dozen or more basic beliefs are buried so deeply in the mind that the average person never recognizes them. Yet they are in every one of us, saint and sinner alike. *These beliefs are molds in which our futures are cast*—even though they remain hidden from sight.

I have given them the name *parent thoughts*, because each of them constantly gives birth to "children." We see the children, rarely the parent. The children are the unhappy experiences that show themselves in our affairs. Not children of chance, but children of very definite parents.

In the past man has attempted to destroy the "children," leaving the "parent" to bear more. One of the purposes of this book is to reveal and unmask the *parent thoughts*. When this is done they bear no more children. This is the only method of bringing about permanent healing, whether it be of a sick body, a sick heart, a sick pocketbook, or a sick business. When this is understood, man is able to move rapidly to the place where he becomes, as William James put it, "consciously right, superior, and happy."

Mr. Bludgin had never feared nor expected ulcers, but he had nurtured a prolific *parent thought* of *irritation*. He was an impatient man, a driver, an explosive fellow. Physical treatment of a physical ulcer would have only been an attempt to destroy the baby. This is why such conditions often stubbornly resist even the most skillful treatment, or return when the treatment is concluded. The basic cause of the ulcer is hidden deep in the thought life. It must be uprooted or dissolved. Happily, there are techniques for doing this.

How a Parent Thought Works

The first thing the individual must learn is that man thinks not only with his brain, but with every cell of his body. Each cell is a center of intelligence. But the intelligence that thinks within the cell is of the same type, quality, and *coloration* as that within the brain. Therefore, whatever issues from the brain must become the pattern of the cell's thinking, for the cell has no power to think independently. The cell is only a receptor.

The person who works under the drive of irritation sends waves of an inflammatory nature coursing along the nerve paths to every part of the body. He is expressing the *parent image* of irritation. Every type of thought must find outlet somewhere. These irritating waves of thought bathing the cells impart their own quality to those cells, which are unable to offer resistance. This steady day-by-day play upon them gradually irritates, then inflames, and finally breaks down the mucosa of the stomach. The result: an ulcer.

True, Mr. Bludgin had never expected nor feared an ulcer. He was too busy with his inflammatory thoughts about the stupidity, the slowness, the laxity of his employees. He did not know what he was doing to himself, but every nerve and fiber of his body knew. He was practicing his belief in the *parent thought* of irritation.

Mr. Bludgin had to be shown that *nothing in the universe possessed the power to irritate him without his consent.* Persons, places, and things never irritate us; it is our *reaction* to them that is irritative.

A person is faced with a certain experience; this becomes a stimulus. A stimulus has no irritating power in itself, but the person can give it the power of irritating him. Or, if he chooses, his response can be one of imperturbable serenity—in which case there is no track along which irritation can flow. The prince of this world findeth nothing in him.

Each person possesses the power to respond or not to respond, as we shall see later. Some react constructively, some destructively. In the last analysis, man is the master of his fate, the captain of his soul.

The Problem of Mastery

An illustration might clarify this point. Three persons live in adjoining apartments. The one in the middle plays her radio loudly all day. Her neighbors meet in the hallway. *A* says to *C*, "That radio drives me crazy. I'm afraid I'm going to walk in one day and throw it out the window. It's making me a nervous wreck." *C* smiles and says, "It doesn't bother me at all. In fact, I sometimes enjoy listening to her programs through the wall." It is the same radio, but two opposite reactions. If the radio in itself were the irritant, both ladies would be equally upset by it. The radio in itself *has* no power to irritate.

21

A might move to another locality. But this would not solve her problem. For she has only dealt with the "child," leaving the *parent thought* to produce more offspring. In the new place something else would irritate her. It might be the mailman, or the grocery clerk, or her neighbor's outlandish hats, or the way the doorman greets her.

This woman might go through some mental gymnastics to render herself immune to the effect of the radio. But until she learns how to dissolve out the irritation *parent thought* she will go through life under its control. She will find a new serenity when she learns how to move onto a level of thinking that is far above *all* belief in the power of anything outside herself to irritate her.

This in turn will remove the sting from situations that formerly bothered or outraged her, will lessen the frequency of their appearance, and will eventually cause her to see what a nuisance she herself must have been to others.

Psychologists tell us that there are two possible reactions to disagreeable experiences: fight or flight. When primitive man found himself suddenly confronted by a snarling animal his body immediately went on an emergency footing. The adrenal glands poured their hormone into his blood, adding to his physical power so that he could fight or run as his judgment dictated. In civilized life the type of danger has changed but the instinctive reaction is the same: we run away or we fight. Neither method is completely satisfactory.

But there is a third possible reaction—transcendence. We can transcend or rise above the condition. One can so divorce himself from both the fear of and the hatred for an irritating or fearful situation that he can rob it of its power to hurt him.

The conversation with Mr. Bludgin became a two-hour interview, too long to be detailed here. The net result was that he was shown the mistake of trying to fight down his irritations when they arose. He was shown that these were only the babies. He had to deal with the parent. To do this he had to go further back and lay the foundation for *master thoughts*. *Master thoughts* are constructively opposed to the destructive *parent thoughts* and will master them.

Mr. Bludgin said, "I've tried to control my outbursts, but I lash out before I know it. I try to put the irritating person or thing out of my mind. I try not to think of it, but it's no use. What am I to do?"

It would have been useless to say, "Just don't think of it." He had tried this for years, but his belief in the power of something outside himself to irritate him was dominant in his thinking, and constantly asserted itself. He was shown that it is much more important what we turn *to* than what we try to turn *from*.

I showed him that man has a Godlike nature buried far beneath his human nature. His shame over his outbursts indicated this. His desire for poise arose from some deep untapped well of tranquillity that was part of his spiritual self. The very fact that he preferred an experience of serenity was proof that he could achieve it, for whatever the mind can conceive it can achieve. But it would have to be brought to the surface by the same law by which his impatience had been developed.

He was brought to see that his impatience was only a bad mental habit. He was not born impatient. All children are born with sweet, lovable natures. But through faulty home or school training he had been allowed to have his own way, his tantrums had not been checked or guided into constructive channels. He had found that he got what he wanted by making a fuss. This gradually became deeply imbedded in the lower depths of his mind and eventually emerged as a definite trait of his personality. It was not his true self, but an excrescence that blighted his Godlike nature. Since it was not a real part of him, it was not necessarily permanent.

"Yes, yes," he said. "I can see that. But the big question with me is, how can I get rid of it? I've taken fifty years to develop it. I haven't got fifty more years to get rid of it."

We showed him that he did not need fifty years. It could be done quickly; in fact, could show results almost immediately.

The Power that Is Beyond Irritation

Mr. Bludgin was impatient to begin. I said, "Very well. What is the most peaceful scene you can ever remember seeing?"

"That's easy. I see it every evening. It's the view from my home. We're on a high promontory overlooking the Pacific. Every day, when I get back from the office, I sit on the front porch with a long, cool highball in my hand. I like to look out over the ocean and watch the sun.

"The sun is very interesting when it sets. Sometimes it seems to pinch in at the center, like a cell dividing. It

24

then gradually assumes the shape of a great golden urn. This changes again and just before it disappears it becomes a crescent moon in reverse. It is so peaceful that it makes me ashamed of myself. And right now as I describe it I can feel all the strain going out of me."

"Good. Let's start with that! Can you ever imagine that sun becoming irritated? Is there anything anywhere that can spoil its tranquillity? Can you imagine it impatiently rushing into the ocean? No, it takes its unhurried time day after day, through wars, famine, depressions, and booms. When the stock market is tumbling, when the market is frantically rising, that sun is still the unhurried picture of peace and quiet beauty.

"That sun cannot think and decide to go places. It is controlled in its movement by the hand of God, isn't it? We can deduce something of the nature of God from His handiwork. Then we can safely assume that the Mind of God is forever at peace with Itself.

"And you, made in the image and likeness of God, partake of that same quality of peace. Hidden deeply in your nature is the same capacity, but you've replaced it by a false belief about yourself. You've believed that you are being pushed and crowded by things outside of yourself. Nothing is crowding you except your own faulty thought habits."

The Eternal within You

"I'm going to make a suggestion: This evening, as you watch that sunset, quietly, very quietly, say to yourself, 'I am part and parcel of this beautiful universe, part of that silent sun, part of the Infinite hand of love that guides it on its way. Deep within me that which is like God responds to that which is operated by God. The unhurried tranquillity of the Eternal is part of my true nature.' "

Mr. Bludgin objected:

"But I have watched that sunset for years and it has not made me less irritable."

"That is because you have never definitely associated *yourself* with it. You have seen it as a phenomenon of nature, a thing of beauty in itself, something *apart* from you. You have admired it, experienced a temporary suggestion of peace, but never allowed yourself to be drawn through it into a personal relationship with its Creator.

"When David the sheepherder lay on his back entranced by the beauty of the starry heavens he said more than 'How beautiful!' It drew him into communion with that which lay beyond this beauty, and in a mystical moment he burst forth with, 'The heavens declare the glory of God and the firmament showeth His handiwork.' To others they showed beauty; to the mystic they showed God.

"All of us are mystics at heart. When one becomes aware of a deeper meaning behind that which appears on the surface he is contemplating it mystically. But we are afraid of the word *mystic*. It connotes either a charlatan gazing at a crystal ball, or a weird creature with sandals, beard, and white robe living in a cave on a mountainside. This is the wrong picture.

"A mystic is one who penetrates the outer material world of sensations and finds his way into the inner world of reality. In this inner world higher laws prevail. Here is the fountainhead of life. Here is our world of causation.

"From this hidden spiritual center life takes its rise. If man is ever to conquer his moods it must be done by sinking his roots deeper into the unseen. This is what is meant by coming to know God. We watch the wonders of this marvelous universe, the smile of an infant, the unfolding of a flower, the beauty of a bird on the wing, the earth bursting into life in the spring. To most people these phenomena bring a certain esthetic pleasure. But our mystic sense tells us more than this; it tells us that these are the play of God on things. We find God through His handiwork as well as through the sacred writings.

"Our minds have a valuable faculty which might be stated thus: That which we consciously *select* in our reasoning mind tends to recede into our deeper levels of mind where it is gradually molded into the stuff of character. The capacious depths of what the psychologists call man's subjective mind is the great fabricating area where the Infinite Artisan ceaselessly turns thoughts into things; therefore, if you will begin to make conscious *selection* of that which you wish to become, it will eventually show forth in your life. This is a *law* of mind; it will not fail you; trust it.

"In the past you have thought of Him in a theological sense, holy, awesome, distant, separated from you. He may be all this. But definitely take up this personal view; make Him close, intimate, within you. As the poet has said, 'Closer is He than breathing and nearer than hands or feet.'

"Coming to know God is not a mysterious exercise. You are a practical businessman. You know that your workmen must be taught the techniques of their trade. Then they practice them. What they call 'gaining experience' is in reality coming to the place where the techniques that at first they consciously selected and tried to learn in their conscious minds become fabricated in their deeper mind into a habit.

"They have not only developed the techniques; they now may be said to have the underlying 'consciousness' of the work. Man can develop a 'consciousness of God' in the same way. The Bible says that man can grow in the knowledge of God."

"But I've lost faith in churches. I don't go there any more. Now you're talking God to me. Soon you'll be trying to get me to attend church. Then I'll have to give up drinking and cussing."

"You probably lost faith in the church because you first lost faith in yourself. But I'm not interested in whether you go to church or not. I'm interested in seeing you well. What you give up depends entirely upon yourself. Giving up anything under compulsion is never righteousness. Every one has an inner light that tells him what is proper. It has been called the law of God written on the heart.

"As one grows in his sense of the inner beauty of things he comes to the place where he knows whether any act is in line with his sense of beauty or not. If it is not, he will give it up himself without being told, and will feel no clinging to it. His inner self comes to know truth, goodness, and beauty to be the highest values; these values are eternal in the human race. If any act does not violate these in his mind he does not have to give it up. The important thing is that one start building a new concept of himself as being part and parcel of all that is.

"He enters into a friendly partnership with God

through what he can see of God's operations in the universe. This is the beginning of his healing, for as he comes to sense his oneness with God he begins to experience the qualities that he attributes to God. Certainly peace, tranquillity, and freedom from irritation are among these."

Don't Believe It—Try It

"A truth can be a truth even though one does not believe it. Man is partaker of the divine nature, whether he assents or not. His belief or disbelief doesn't change it. But he can prove it to himself by putting it to the test. Suppose you take just seven days to put this to the test. Follow the method I have suggested and let me know the results."

Mr. Bludgin shook his head. "I'm willing to try. But I doubt that it will do much good, because I won't be really believing it. I'm not convinced yet, by any means."

"Do it anyway for seven days adding the words *'This is the truth about me whether I believe it or not.'* You may not have a gigantic faith. But the very fact that you do it will indicate at least a faith as large as a grain of mustard seed. And we've been told that even this much can remove mountains."

Our friend came back in a week, his face like the rising sun. "Where have you been all my life? Why haven't I stumbled onto this before? I don't know whether I still have an ulcer, but I'm surely having fun and I feel good inside.

"We have a new kitten at our house. I sat the other evening and watched it play with a ball. Its quickness, its grace, and the fact that it seemed to be having fun in-

29

trigued me. Then I thought, 'Why not tie this in with my new idea?' So I quietly said, 'The Mind of God is moving through all this kitten's activities. Somewhere in me that same Mind operates with ease, grace, and pleasure.'

"I've always taken great pleasure in my roses as things of beauty. But this week I've taken to seeing them mystically. I noticed their delicate shadings of color, their engineering structure, their rich fragrance, and I said, 'The thought of God is in each one, planning, constructing its form, distilling these fragrant essences from soil, water, and sun. In me likewise this same Mind is trying to bring forth the forms of beauty and pleasantness.'

"I've watched the purple shadows steal across the mountains behind the house, and the stillness of the ocean at morning. I've tried to capture David's reaction to the nightly stars. I've caught the spirit behind the song of the birds in the fruit trees, the humming of the bees. In fact, I'm rediscovering the world I live in. It's a storehouse of beauty."

A few weeks later his wife telephoned me and said, "What have you done to Mr. Bludgin? Now I have the kind of man I fell in love with twenty-five years ago, and the girls at the office tell me that he is so gracious now that they're wondering if he might be ill."

This was seven years ago. His ulcer has long since departed because that which caused it has gone. The threatened surgery was never needed. But better still, that man now lives as he was intended to live, freed from a mistaken notion that persons, places, or things have any power to irritate him without his consent.

ALL OF LIFE'S ILLS
COME FROM

PARENT THOUGHTS

They are the basic beliefs that dominate your life, *whether you are aware of them or not.*

There is no use in battling the illnesses of the troubles themselves, for when the present ones are gone the PARENT THOUGHTS will produce more.

YOU MUST CULTIVATE

MASTER THOUGHTS

They are the positive, constructive beliefs that will root out the trouble-making parent thoughts and allow Creative Law to operate.

chapter three

The Universe Needs You

NEWSPAPERS AND MAGAZINES TODAY ARE TELLING OF THE remarkable results being obtained through *psychosomatic* medicine. The term is derived from two Greek words—*psyche*, meaning mind or soul, and *soma*, meaning body. *Psychosomatic* refers to the intimate relationship existing between the way a person thinks and the way his body behaves.

For centuries this aspect of man's affairs was ignored by most medical men or treated with scorn as a cultish notion. But a striking change has come over the scientific world during the past generation.

From the time of Hippocrates, doctors have been puzzled by the occasional complete cure of a person without the intervention of any material treatment. The more thoughtful physicians in every century carried on desul-

31

tory research into the question. But in the past few decades they have taken off their coats and really gone to work. In private offices, clinics, and hospitals they have painstakingly probed the minds of their patients, building up an ever-growing body of knowledge on the subject. By constant laboratory checks, they have made this knowledge more and more exact.

Perhaps the best-known exponent of psychosomatic views is Flanders Dunbar, M.D., formerly vice-president of the American Psychopathological Association and editor-in-chief of the *Journal of Psychosomatic Medicine*. Through the painstaking research carried on by Dr. Dunbar and her colleagues in Presbyterian Hospital, New York, Massachusetts General Hospital, Boston, and other reputable institutions, this interrelationship of thought with physical disorders has been placed on the basis of scientific scholarship. Her work has been augmented by a host of other eminent medical authorities working separately; their names are to be found in the literature of psychosomatic medicine.

These studies leave no doubt that body and mind are inextricably intermeshed. It is impossible to establish a point at which body leaves off and mind begins, or vice versa. The action of one seems automatically to become the action of the other.

In the past, there were always a number of borderline disorders that were considered to be chiefly of the mind, if not purely imaginary. Neurasthenia in its various forms, some types of indigestion, certain palpitations of the heart, and various hypertensions had long been suspected of being emotional in origin.

Today the list has broadened considerably to include such apparently organic illnesses as bronchial asthma, arthritis, hay fever, heart disease, gastric ulcer, mucous colitis, diabetes mellitus, tuberculosis, dental caries, cancer, paralysis, and eczema.

The register is being increased every month. It is not beyond the realm of possibility that some day every illness of man will be proved to arise out of his own worried, confused, disintegrated, deeply buried emotional states. That which once was called the disease is now being seen to be only the outward and visible symptom, the disease itself being the distorted thought life of the patient.

The conviction is steadily growing that healing, if it is to be permanent and thorough, must be the healing of the disordered mental patterns. Where this is done, patients are being brought daily into a new world, that of the superior mind producing a superior body. A world-famous surgeon was asked what the surgeon of the twenty-first century would be like; it was not levity that impelled him to reply, "There will be no surgeons."

States of Mind That Cause Accidents

Some may find it difficult to credit the fact that accidents arise from personality states. But Dr. Dunbar shows that there is a definite "accident-prone" type. In fact, psychosomatic medicine has progressed so far that it can almost predict the kind of trouble a person is likely to have by a study of his personality. This is an approach to our theory of *parent thoughts*.

Figures don't lie. Here is the story. A large public utility was concerned over the prevalence of accidents among its drivers. In spite of severe penalties, the high accident rate continued. Men with bad accident rates were moved to indoor jobs, and the accident rate went down. But the drivers moved inside still had "accidentitis." They had accidents with the machinery, in their homes, in athletics; in fact, wherever they went.

The type was studied. He takes very good care of his own health, is ill much less than the average person. His sex activities are somewhat promiscuous, yet he has less venereal trouble. He has a decisiveness to an almost trigger-like degree. Immediate pleasures have more attraction for him than remote goals.

At first sight, these traits seem to indicate a person who would respond quickly and favorably to the problems of safe driving. But there are other connected traits more deeply buried. It is the hidden attitudes that are the most powerful and that cause the trouble.

The accident-prone man has an extreme resentment of authority. He has feelings of rebellion against pressures of church, law, relatives, parents, partners. These feelings are often unconscious until his attention is directed to them.

How the Parent Thought of Separation Works

The basic *parent thought* underlying the accident habit is that of *separation*.

We do not resent the necessary pressures of the group to which we belong because we feel one with them. The anti-social individual does not feel one with his family or his fellows. He resents their pressures. He stands as one apart. He stifles the natural warm outgoingness of the normal person and gives little of himself to those near him.

34

Dr. Dunbar points out that the underlying thought patterns of the accident-prone person and of the criminal are similar. The one unconsciously takes it out on society; the other unconsciously punishes himself through accidents.

The consequences, too, are similar. One suffers separation from society in prison; the other in a hospital, with fractures, dislocations, or torn ligaments—all of which are separations.

The *parent thought* of separation operates in other fields. It brings about jiltings, desertions, loss of jobs, broken friendships, and a host of other situations in which one becomes separated from that to which he wishes to remain attached.

The person so deprived rarely recognizes the real cause of the tragedy. He blames the perfidy of friends, the ingratitude of an employer, the whispering or talebearing of a third party. The reluctantly separated person becomes the woman-hater or the man-hater. All he can see is the immediate cause of his trouble. He will "never trust another person as long as he lives." "Never again will I throw everything of myself into a job; when the boss is through with you, he'll toss you away like a squeezed orange." He becomes sour, cynical, bitter. The pity of it is that he will go down to his grave still muttering of the baseness of his fellows unless he is brought to see that the entire thing started within himself.

Sooner or later all of us are treated as we deserve. This may sound harsh or callous, but it is gospel truth. This law of cause-and-effect knows nothing but constantly to produce effects out of their corresponding causes. Once

35

we establish this as a guiding principle of life, we will never again be guilty of saying, "*Why* has this experience come upon me?" or "*Why* do people do thus or so to me?" The emphasis shifts from *why* to *what*. "*What* in me is stirring this up in them?"

This is the way of deliverance, of escape, of healing. The reason why many people continue to lead disappointed lives, to suffer chronically from illness, to fail when everything in the universe is willing to cooperate in their success, is because they are looking in the wrong place for the cause of their unhappy condition.

The Universe Thinks Unity

One of the basic *master thoughts* of the universe is that of unity. The word *universe* is from two Latin words meaning "to turn into one." It depicts *one* coherent, cooperating system, achieving unity out of diversity.

Basically, all men are One Big Man. Each of us is only a single cell in the great body of humanity. We find a parallel in the remarkable cooperative interaction of the trillions of cells in our bodies, by means of whch each does its own work, yet always seems to be providing beneficent substances and opportunities for the others to develop.

There is a unity of action by which the sun draws the moisture from the earth and returns it as rain; in the nitrogen cycle by which bacteria disintegrate dead materials and return the nitrogen for our use. Without such cycles the earth would become a dead planet devoid of plant and animal life. Look as far as we can in every direction, the universe proclaims its oneness with ten million voices.

Many persons practice daily the belief in separation

36

without ever being aware of it. Good will is unity; ill will is separation. Love is unity; hate is separation. A smile is unity; a frown is separation. Praise is unity; nagging is separation. Laughter is unity; tears are separation. Hope is unity; despair is separation. Generous congratulation is unity; silent envy is separation. Trust is unity; jealousy is separation.

Man's Hunger for Reunion

There is no such person as an atheist. Some call themselves atheists for some reason quite external to their spiritual selves. This one is an atheist because his scientific studies have led him to believe that the universe is a vast mechanism running by blind chance. That one calls himself an atheist because in childhood he prayed that his little brother would not die, but he died in spite of the prayer. The other says he is an atheist because his political philosophy calls for atheism.

These men are all atheists of the intellect. No one is an atheist of the heart and spirit; it is impossible. At birth each has built into him an eternal hunger for reunion with his Maker. Some recognize it early in life; others later; some never at all. But it is there nevertheless.

Many of the hungers that are attributed to unsatisfied ambition are cries of the inner spiritual self. As the physical body cries for physical food, so the spirit of man can never be satisfied without spiritual sustenance from his Creator.

Rufus Jones has said that man has invisible spiritual antennae that quest forever into the unseen. But he insists that man does not start that search. A double search is forever going on so that Spirit with spirit can meet. The Infinite is questing for an expressional outlet through man; man receives these impressions as earthlings might register signals from some distant planet, not knowing what they are. When he recognizes them, union can take place.

As mentioned earlier, this union can take place through many different avenues. The nature lover, enthralled by the sublime beauty of a sunset, might feel completely empty and lifeless in a church, yet he comes alive standing beside a rippling stream arched over by beautiful trees, the rich, clean smell of the earth in his nostrils. These he can understand; theology he cannot. This, then, is the place from which to start.

No one should ever be expected to violate his own reasoning processes, to accept theological dogma from which his type of mind shrinks. Union with God is something far larger than church membership.

Another man sees little to enrapture him in nature. His philosophic or doctrinal type of mind easily grasps abstruse theological formulae. He feels perfectly at home in the church; it gives him a sense of union with God. He belongs there. But he should not berate our first man whose spiritual perceptions would be unawakened in church.

I had a friend, a brilliant engineer whose record of accomplishment had brought him great wealth and high honors. For some years before he passed on, he was on the board of trustees of the highly scientific California Institute of Technology. Walking about his beautiful estate in Bel Air one afternoon, with this tall, erect man nearing eighty, I asked him about the faith of a scientist.

He stopped, plucked a flower, a sweet pea, and said,

"A chemist can make this fragrance synthetically. He can even tell to a certain degree the process by which the scent was developed in nature. A plastics operator can make a flower as beautiful as this. But science cannot yet make a living sweet pea. My faith rests upon the fact that this flower has a matchless Maker.

"This is an intellectual concept. But in the long silent nights, when I was a mining engineer out on the African desert, I would ponder these things, and an indescribable sense of peace would steal into me. It then became a thing of the heart rather than the intellect. It seemed as if the Creator were nodding his head at my musings and that both He and I and the universe were all part of each other.

"This is my faith. I am a member and a supporter of the church, but if my pastor were to tell me I must throw this faith away and take on one of words and doctrines, I would never enter his church again."

After all, the purpose of all doctrines is to lead men closer to God; this is the expressed purpose of the church. The man who is led into a sense of close union with God through contemplating a flower or the heavens would seem to have as valid a union as he who has come through theology. As the church comes more and more to teach its theological message by illustrations and deductions, drawn from the hand of God in this marvelous universe, it will attract many who now wrongly think that they are atheists.

> Not understood, we move along asunder;
> Our paths grow wider as the seasons creep
> Along the years; we marvel and we wonder

Why life is life, and then we fall asleep
Not understood.

Ah God! that men would see a little clearer,
Or judge less harshly where they cannot see!
Ah God! that men would draw a little nearer
To one another—they'd be nearer Thee,
And understood.

Thomas Bracken

To Reunite Is to Heal

I have dealt with specific problems. But all problems
are forms of separation from the ideal perfection. It is
not important at this point whether this perfection is
thought of as an impersonal Absolute or as Personal God
and Father.

Vivid awareness of perfection might be engendered
by the contemplation of beauty, by a true love such as
healed Elizabeth Barrett, or by a sense of the brooding
Presence of the Almighty in the heart. The pictures might
vary; the end result is a reunion with perfection. And to
reunite with perfection is to heal.

Each person must discover the method by which he is
drawn into this union with the perfect. It is interesting
to note that he who comes to it through what might be
called a nonreligious train of thought usually progresses
through this to a very acceptable spiritual concept. He is
led to God through a sequence of thought that fits his
particular type of mind, education, and background. Many
roads lead to the City of God. The particular road is not
important; the destination is all.

Love is a definite healing power. Therefore he who would be healed might start on a practical level. He could begin to praise someone sincerely. One man told me that he had completely recovered from recurrent attacks of shingles after he had started praising his wife for her cooking, her taste in draperies, and other accomplishments that he had always taken for granted, or had criticized.

In a sense, we are cruel to those who love us by our failure to appreciate the various facets of that love. Thoughtlessness has killed love in the hearts of more women than infidelity. The spirit of praise and appreciation has bound people together with bands of steel.

Envy is a killer because it is the practice of separation. When the Bible urges us to "Rejoice with them that rejoice, and weep with them that weep," it is enjoining union as against separation. He who envies is weeping because others rejoice. It is a reversal of the stated principle.

Properly understood, the Bible is the most practical book in the world. It contains every principle of psychosomatic medicine, every principle of business success, every foundation for happy, enduring marriage, every law by which any of us can attain any cherished goal in this present existence. We have been too prone to project its promises to a life on the other side. Every one of them can be fulfilled on this side.

The Right Way to Practice Unity

Earlier we said that a smile is union, a frown is separation. As part of the process of healing, one could commence consciously and deliberately to cultivate the habit of greeting others with a quick, warm smile.

There are right and wrong ways of doing this. The person who sees a card that reads, "Keep Smiling," and follows the advice because it seems to him like a good idea, is doing a good thing, but not the best. He who invests his smile with the knowledge that he is deliberately aligning himself with a new belief in union, in the cultivation of a definite *master thought* to offset his negative parent thought of separation, has taken the better way. He is living by a *principle* rather than a *rule*.

Principles intelligently recognized and practiced have vastly more power than surface rules. They penetrate more thoroughly to deeper mind.

A smile pays an implicit compliment to the person to whom it is given. It is one way of saying, "I like you. I feel close to you," where words conveying the same idea might be thought insincere or at least out of place. From childhood we have associated a smile with union, a frown with separation until it has become a subjective automatic conclusion. We are unconsciously drawn toward the person who smiles at us.

One can practice his belief in union in a thousand little friendlinesses. It does not matter whether these are appreciated. We are trying to re-form our deeper thought patterns to bring them into line with what we believe to be the thinking of the Infinite Thinker. If others return our good will, we are that much ahead; if they do not, we are not cast down. Our chief concern is that we shall destroy our *parent thought* of separation. Our method of doing this is not by fighting the idea of separation, but by practicing union. Not by turning *from* the negative, but by turning *to* the positive.

At this point, something should be said about our general approach to self-mastery. We can better change conditions by turning *to* the desirable rather than by turning *from* the undesirable. Thus, it is better to build a consciousness of health than to fight illness; better to cultivate the consciousness of abundance than to struggle against poverty; better to develop the inner consciousness of loving harmony than to battle against discord.

This was the underlying approach of Jesus to all of man's problems. St. Paul suggested the same approach when he said, "Finally brethren, whatsoever things are true, honest, just, pure, lovely, of good report, think on *these* things." Fill the consciousness with what we want brought forth in our lives rather than with what we want driven out.

One day I picked up a drinking glass that had lain in the garden for some weeks. It was encrusted with dry earth. It could be cleaned in either of two ways. The harder way would have been painstakingly to scrape and scratch and dig that dirt out. I took the easier way. I set it under the warm water faucet, left the water running, and occupied myself with something else for five minutes. When I returned, the glass was spotless. Steadily and easily, the warm water had continued to pour in gradually replacing the dirt. The steady inflow of the beautiful suggested by St. Paul clears out the ugliness of destructive thought.

THE CAUSE OF YOUR UN-HAPPINESS IS WITHIN YOU.

If you try to find it anywhere else, you're *looking in the wrong place.*

For example. The parent thought of *Separation* causes much of life's misery. See how the answers to the troubles caused by it can be found in your own mind and heart, in the master thought of *Unity*.

SEPARATION   UNITY

SEPARATION	UNITY
ill will	*good will*
hate	*love*
a frown	*a smile*
nagging	*praise*
tears	*laughter*
despair	*hope*
silent envy	*generous* *congratulations*

chapter four

Why the Rich Get Richer

IN 1927 I ADDRESSED THE LIONS CLUB OF SACRAMENTO, California. During the luncheon, I was seated beside Warden Smith of Folsom Prison. In the course of the conversation, I told him that I had been preparing a series of articles on the dominant thought patterns of certain groups of people, and that I would like to know something of the working of the criminal mind.

Upon his invitation, I visited this prison, where California's most desperate criminals were incarcerated. We had dinner prepared and served by the inmates. I was particularly impressed by the finely chiseled features and the dignified bearing of one of the waiters. I could not believe that he was an inmate. He seemed to be a man who would be received anywhere. But the warden assured me that his crime was a particularly revolting murder, and that he had previously spent years in other prisons.

For several hours, I was permitted to mingle freely with certain of the inmates. I spent much time with the man who had attracted my attention. His philosophy of life was one that seemed prevalent among the others, but in him it was accompanied by an intense bitterness. He felt that society had denied him a chance, then had persecuted him.

He related the circumstances of his birth. His father had deserted "the old lady" before he was born. He had grown up in the slum section of one of the large cities, had started stealing fruit at the corner vegetable store, and had followed the usual course of a juvenile delinquent—playing hooky, running with the gang, and eventually finding his way into major crime. He was filled with envious hatred of anyone who had succeeded, and he wound up a particularly vitriolic tirade with the words, "The rich get richer and the poor get poorer. What chance does a poor kid have anyway! The only way he can get what he wants is by going wrong."

Income Follows Consciousness

"The rich get richer while the poor get poorer." I agreed with the inmate, telling him that the Great Teacher also agreed with him. Jesus once said, "Unto every one that hath shall be given, but from him that hath not shall be taken away even that which he hath." Like many sayings of the Master this seems to be harsh, but it illustrates the truth He was always trying to teach men.

He had tried to show that a man's thought had power; that it was the alpha and omega of his experience. In this verse He was saying that those who gather more of this world's goods have evidenced a more vigorous money *consciousness*. At this point He did not debate whether wealth was good or bad, or whether the person acquired it rightfully or wrongfully. He merely stated the law of mind by which one draws anything into his experience.

The steady expectancy of money had drawn that money to them. Now they had it. Very well, that same consciousness would draw more of it to them. This law applies to health and to every other good thing for which people yearn. On the other hand, he who has little evidently has an unsound consciousness at this point. Since the law of life is to increase and magnify any state of mind, the path of life will lead downward for the second person.

The first person is moving constantly out into deeper waters of supply. The second moves steadily into shallower waters. The unsound consciousness of the second may be further distorted by seeing the first become richer. If he gives in to envy, hatred, and feelings of persecution, these emotions drain his consciousness still lower, with a resultant lowering of income. A malign fate seems to diminish even the little that he has—but it is his own state of mind that robs him. He has taken into himself the *parent thought* of *futility*.

There are those who have broken away from slum influences, who have never allowed them to infiltrate into their souls. In Jacqueline Cochran's thrilling life story, *The Stars at Noon*, she courageously strips away all pretense and tells the story of her early life, spent amid the most sordid circumstances. Half-starved, half-educated, one might almost say half-civilized, living in the swamps of the southern states, she had something within her that

47

refused to allow the swamps to set their measure upon her. The Law of God written on her heart made her determined to burst the bars of circumstance and grapple with her evil star. Walking out of that unambitious home, she became a proficient beauty operator at thirteen, a trained nurse before she was twenty, and the wife of a millionaire a few years later.

Her flying record speaks for her courage and skill. She has come a long way. Nobody pushed her; her family derided her when as a child she persisted in bathing regularly. It would have been the easiest thing in the world for her to settle down, submit to the pressures, and become a slattern. But she never allowed the slightest feelings of self-pity to enter. She never allowed envy to sear her soul. If others could have the nice things of life, she knew that she could have them too.

Jacqueline Cochran proved that there is something in the human soul that can offset the strongest pressures from the environment. There is a Power within any of us that can lift us to the heights.

It's the Set of the Sails, Not the Gales

Compare Jacqueline Cochran with the prison inmate whom we met at the beginning of this chapter. Here were two people with the same circumstances, but with opposite results, proving that it is not what life does to us, but the way we react, that matters. The one allowed his surroundings to ruin his life; the other used them as steppingstones to bring her to the end of the rainbow.

Each of us has some element in his surroundings upon which thoughts of futility can fasten. Poverty is not

48

the only deadening factor. Wealth has ruined as many as has poverty. One may start life with a frail body, a less-than-brilliant mind, or any one of a dozen defects upon which our lesser selves could pounce, using them as excuses for our failure to mature. "It's the set of the sails, and not the gales, that determines the way each goes." It is something that operates within, rather than the gales that blow from without, that makes the difference between winner and whiner.

"But," someone asks, "how shall I know whether futility dominates me?" One way to know is to watch the reasons we give for our illness, our failure to succeed either in business or in the love life. He who says, "Everything I touch goes wrong no matter what I do or how hard I try" or "People take advantage of me, never co-operate with me," can classify himself without others pointing it out to him. Sometimes the giveaway is, "No doctor can ever find out what my trouble is. I've been to the best and I think that they are all either ignorant or charlatans."

Something Is Always Going Right

It is not true that "everything always goes wrong" with any person. His sense of futility blinds him to the many things that go right. If one would review the events of the day, among the unhappy experiences he could find at least a few that were pleasant.

Men search for gold, but they seldom find it in large nuggets. They carefully pan for tiny specks and flakes. These can be melted into larger nuggets. Our good comes to us usually in this way—occasionally a nugget, but most of the time in little flecks. A cheerful greeting from the newsboy, the smile of a child, a word of compliment or appreciation, a slight improvement in some technical skill, a small order when we would like to have made a big sale, a slight sign of intelligence in some slower student— these are the makings of happiness.

A schoolteacher said: "I have the worst kind of pupils. They are a bunch of little roughnecks. They pay small attention to me. They even giggle contemptuously when they greet me on the grounds. I'm a failure. Everything I do is wrong. I'm sure the other teachers make fun of me behind my back, and I'm afraid that I'll be let out at the end of this school year."

She was encouraged to sit quietly in the schoolroom for fifteen minutes after the children had gone, carefully reviewing the day's work and jotting down anything that seemed to belie what she had said to me, no matter how trivial it might seem at the time. Even if there were only one incident, write it down! Then at home she was to lie down comfortably and let her mind drift back along the events of the day.

There might be only three encouraging things re-membered, but these could make a tiny nugget. She was to give thanks for them and allow them to become a nucleus of happiness, for the next day more would be remembered.

Our minds always see more of anything that we are looking for. We pass by most of the advertisements in the papers, but our eye is caught when we see something we are thinking of buying. That article may have been advertised daily for months, but to us it was not there until our wanting it brought it to our attention.

The schoolteacher's search worked a miracle for her. One child whom she had thought rather stupid crept timidly back into the classroom and asked her a question about the two Presidents named Adams, and thanked her very nicely for her assistance. On the way out another child whose deportment usually left much to be desired was bending over a narrow flower bed. As the teacher passed, she straightened up and said, "Oh, Miss Blue, did you ever see anything so beautiful!" It was the first real commingling of souls between them as they stooped to examine and discuss the flowers. On the bus the driver felt her animation and remarked, "You must have had a good day today. You look happy." To which she replied, "I've had a wonderful day."

It is not necessary to relate the details, but good things began to flow in her direction. The discipline began to improve. The mental level of her pupils seemed to rise. The janitor at her apartment brought her a little scene that his daughter had painted. None of these were big in themselves, but they certainly grew out of her redirected awareness.

Our Fortune Begins within Us

In one sense, none of us ever has a chance except the chance he makes for himself. Inherited wealth or a brilliant mind will do nothing for one unless he cultivates the ability to make effective use of them. Heaven and hell have their origins within the human heart. No one is ever condemned by any power outside himself. *We* condemn ourselves to a life of frustration. The tragedy is that so often we fail to see where the mainsprings of experience lie. We think they are outside us when they are within.

This mistaken view of life may never lead one to criminality, but it can ruin his chances for happiness. It can hold one in the shackles of the *parent thought* of futility, where the will to win almost disappears. We stress the word *almost*, because "hope springs eternal within the human breast." It can be smothered; its light may flicker and grow dim, but in the proper circumstances it can be fanned into a bright flame.

A real estate salesman said: "I work hard. I do the best I can. But I have not closed a sale in six months." He worked in an active district; other salesmen in the same office were closing deals. He was not physically lazy. The evidence was that somewhere in the recesses of his deeper mind he did not *want* to close sales.

At first, he was hurt and angry when this was pointed out to him, but he was brought to the place where he was willing to admit its possibility. Questioning revealed that his divorced wife had been making demands upon him for an increase in her support. This he was not willing to grant. In order to support his argument that he was unable to increase the amount, he had let several sales slide six months before. He had thought that by making a poor showing he would be able to present her with evidence that would cause her to desist from her demands.

The deeper mind has a curious way of turning an action into a habit if this action is accompanied by a strong emotion. In his case, he had hated his ex-wife, had told friends he would starve before he would give her any more money. Whenever he thought of a way to outwit her, he felt very strongly about it.

It is impossible to hold ugliness in one corner of the mind without its coloring the entire thinking process. This man had a duty to provide for his ex-wife who was living in squalid surroundings, subsisting on the bare necessities. By determining to hold her good away from her, he was unwittingly expressing a belief that one's good can be withheld without that person's consent. Whatever one believes about another, he unconsciously believes about himself; therefore, this thought began operating in all sections of his mind and closed down on his sales.

The only thing that can happen to us is that in which we believe. This is the reason why the Golden Rule is not only kind to others, but is good practical living for ourselves. When we interfere with the good of another, we thereby open the door for someone else to interfere with our good.

It is not necessary for others to know of our infractions of mental law. The law itself knows and acts as a principle of reflection, fulfilling itself in our affairs. The prospects whom our salesman contacted knew nothing of his domestic affairs, but the law kept on working quite impersonally and the customers were not impressed with his sales arguments. His own belief was fulfilling itself.

What a person is he is to the bottom of himself and with all of himself. He may separate his external self from his inner self in order to impress his friends, but the law of his own mind knows nothing of such a separation. All it knows is to fabricate the totality of his thought into form.

This man was puzzled and confused. He felt that something was unfair. If he had known and understood the law of his thought life, he would have been able to put his finger on the difficulty immediately. Nothing was blocking his prosperity but his own thought. He had thought that he had "lost his punch," and he did not know where to look for it. His "punch" had never been his. It had been the working of the Creative Process on a mind focused to one point: the selling of property. Now he had become the "double-minded man unstable in all his ways," and the negative belief about life had assumed dominance.

He was brought to the place where he saw that hate will always destroy the contact with Infinite Love, and that no one who hates can ever be truly happy. I left the matter of providing for his ex-wife in the background and concentrated on the idea of his aligning himself with those qualities of God that could be traced. Especially I stressed love.

I have seldom seen a man so thoroughly transformed. It could truly be said that he had been born again. He was a new, a different person. He became one of the most gracious of men and his graciousness was genuine.

Of course, sales came faster for this man. As they did, he increased his allowance to his ex-wife.

There was an interesting outcome to this case. At about the time he got rid of his hostility for his ex-wife, she met another man who swept her off her feet in a whirl-wind courtship and they were married within three months. Her second husband was a successful businessman who assured the real estate man he was well able to provide fully for his new wife. Thus two problems were settled at the same time.

Where Does the Dead Cat Belong?

"The rich get richer; the poor get poorer." Political ideologies have been built up on misinterpretations of this fact of life. Lives have been spent in the shallows of futility. The acids of frustration and envy have eaten away at the happiness of millions who have believed that the rich were lucky and the poor were underprivileged. Politicians have ridden into power on this lie, exploiting it for their own benefit, cooing their sympathy for the blinded souls who voted them in. Encouraged to suck on a governmental breast, the "underprivileged" have been kept in political and spiritual infancy.

The time has come to lay the dead cat on the only doorstep where it belongs: at the feet of the individual. Each of us must learn that the key to every man is his thought, that it is done unto him according to his own belief. If he continues to believe a lie, he will continue to experience the false and unsatisfying life that issues from that lie.

No dictator, no politician can give a man anything more than his own consciousness draws in. All they can give is a political system. Within that system, each of us can garner only that which is the reproduction of his own consciousness. They who have not the consciousness remain the slaves under any system. The cream will always rise to the top; it always has. This is not one of man's laws. It is a law of God, working through man's mental operations.

"The rich get richer; the poor get poorer." Truer word was never spoken. But it is a statement of mental law—not an edict of God. The riches are the riches of consciousness.

HAVING ENOUGH, WHERE MONEY IS CONCERNED, IS UP TO YOU

If the lack of money is the source of your troubles, you are bringing them on yourself, because you are allowing the parent thought of

FUTILITY

to dominate your thinking.

Your fortune begins with you. *Believe* you can handle money matters, *believe* you will have what you need.

You are CONFIDENT.

You are RESOURCEFUL.

Carry these master thoughts in your mind and the details of your finances will straighten out. The Creative Process is working for you NOW.

chapter five

Why Choose Fear?

THE STORY IS TOLD OF THE WISE OLD MAN SITTING BE-
neath a tree in India. The spirit of the plague went by.
"Whither goest thou?" the wise man asked. "I go to
Benares, where I shall slay one hundred persons," was the
reply. Three months later, the spirit of the plague again
passed the wise man on its return journey. "You said you
would slay one hundred in Benares, but travelers tell me
you slew ten thousand," said the wise man. To which the
spirit of the plague replied, "I slew but one hundred. Fear
slew the others."

As one learns to be at home in the spiritual and mental
world, all of his fears lessen and with the lessening of fear
comes a lessening of the effects of fear. I suppose that all
of us have twinges around the heart at times or some dis-
concerting symptom in the back or elsewhere. Instead of

rushing off to the doctor expecting to hear the worst, the wise person inhibits this rising tide of panic, quietly declares that by the Law of Right Action nothing destructive can operate in him, turns in mind to the idea of an Infinite Perfection within and surrounding him, and quietly goes about his business, releasing himself—spirit, mind, and body —to the beneficent Creative Law. Usually it is days later that he recalls he had a passing twinge.

The Fearful Mind Tempts Providence

I have a vivid picture of a woman in mind. She was one of the most fear-ridden persons I have ever encountered, yet she was a fine person at heart. She was completely self-centered and neurotic. She had bought every aid to health advertised by radio, television, and newspaper. She had vibrating belts, easy reducing pills, and upsidedown boards to lie on. She had exhausted the patience of several doctors; had gone from medical to drugless methods; and now was convinced that "faith healing"—as she called it—was the only thing that could save her.

Her first words were, "Dr. Bailes, I am a very sick woman, and these doctors are all frauds. All they want is my money and they do nothing for me. You are my last hope. If you cannot heal me, I'm at the end of my rope."

"Then you are in a bad situation," I replied, "because I have no power to heal anyone."

"You are just being modest. I know that you are a faith healer because you healed my brother-in-law of diabetes."

"May I correct you on two points? In the first place, a faith healer is one who claims to have a healing gift.

58

People have faith in his peculiar gift and any benefit they receive comes from their faith in him, without any intelligent understanding of the process involved. I have no gift of healing. I can heal no one. In the second place, when your brother-in-law was healed, it was not by me. It was by his own changed attitudes toward life. You too can be healed, but the entire transaction will have to take place within your own mind.

"Spiritual healing is quite different from faith healing. It rests on no person, but on a Law of Healing. This Law cannot operate for you as long as you spend your whole time feeling your pulse and listening to your arteries harden. You have a companion who drives your car because you say that you are afraid you will faint or have a heart attack in traffic. Have you ever fainted?"

"No. But, I am afraid that some day I will. One of my doctors said . . ."

"Mrs. Tremble, do you think you could learn to say, 'So what!' Could you bring yourself to the point where you did not give a snap of your fingers whether you fainted or even died at the wheel of your car? Could you say to every flutter and palpitation of your heart, to every shortness of breath, to every feeling of distress at any point in your body, 'You are a bluffer; you are nothing trying to be something. You are a nonexistent bogey man hiding under the bed; you are a child of my imagination. Come on, do your worst, for from now on I'm going to laugh in your face.' Do you think you could take such a stand?"

"But, Dr. Bailes, that would be tempting Providence. And I really *do* have a bad heart."

"You are tempting Providence now by your constant

brooding over your condition. We shall not debate the reality or otherwise of your symptoms. You say that you have been doctoring for thirteen years, and getting worse all the time. You could not get much worse if you said, 'So what! If I die I die, and I am not going to die daily in anticipation of it.' Remember, the fear of dying is the surest road to dying."

The Healing Power of "So What!"

We talked for more than an hour. Finally she said, "Do you know, I rather like this idea of snapping my fingers in death's face. For thirteen years that fear has hounded me. I think it is time I turned the tables."

This type of person does not usually accept this new idea so readily. But she was made of good stuff; all she needed was someone to give her a different slant on life.

She got into her car, drove it home herself, went through the house tossing nostrums into the wastebasket, and declared her independence. That fall she joined a nine-month class I was forming for the deeper study of these principles. She became one of the finest practitioners of the Healing Law that I have ever seen. Incidentally, she reduced forty pounds during that class, without her nostrums.

Fear Is Developed, Not Inborn

Psychologists tell us that fear is not an inheritance. Infants enter the world with only two fears, neither of which causes much trouble in later life. They fear a sudden loud noise and they fear being dropped. But every other fear that drives us has been built up during our lifetime. We create Frankenstein-monsters and the monsters

60

pursue us throughout life. As soon as we learn that fear is nothing but a bad mental habit and that we are quite capable of developing new habits of courage, we are on the pathway to deliverance.

The conquest of fear is the conquest of disease, for the latter is largely the child of the former. Destroy the cause and the effect dies of itself. The very simplicity of this statement is a barrier to its acceptance. People stubbornly look for some complicated theory when the answer is in fact quite simple.

The Right Picture Becomes the Right Reality

In my discussion with Mrs. Tremble, I stressed the fact that our minds are like picture galleries. Old pictures are constantly being taken down and new ones put up. The mind never carries the same pictures permanently. Some stay longer than others. Some seem to stay throughout life, yet there is always a constant, even a momentary changing of pictures.

The body is momentarily reflecting the pictures on the walls of the mind. The Creative Law is momentarily assuming new forms and momentarily dissolving the old forms. For this reason, we pay scant attention to any given form. That which might cause panic in one ignorant of this Law causes no ripple of excitement in the person who knows the truth. He holds quietly to the knowledge that any form in which destructiveness is operating must disappear when the fundamental harmony is re-established. He is not afraid of it because he knows that it is out of tune with the Infinite Constructiveness.

When one can look a frightening situation in the face

61

and deny that it has any law to support it, he has made progress. When he can go further and confidently affirm that he knows the Power that can change it, he has gone higher. When he can say that his word can direct that Force into operation at this particular point, he has arrived at the point Jesus spoke of. "Ye shall *know* the truth, and the truth shall set you free."

"But, how long does it take to reach this third stage?" It is not a matter of time, but of consciousness. I have received letters telling that before the readers had finished one of my books, they had come into complete and permanent healing. Some cling more stubbornly to outworn prejudices. But anyone can understand and start applying the principle by the time he has read this book.

Drunken, dissipated criminals have gone into rescue missions in the Skid Rows of various cities. During the one hour of the service, they have completely revolutionized their thinking and have gone out to become sober, respected citizens of the community. That is how fast one's whole outlook on life can change. It does not take months or years to grasp an idea if the person is really serious in his desire for a new life. Some fight alcohol for years. The rescue missions have hundreds of men who have lost the desire and appetite for it in an hour. So it is with one's awakening to the tremendous force of the Infinite Creative Power.

Put Up the Right Picture Right Now

May we suggest that the reader stop right here, select some person, perhaps himself, who needs help. Let him quietly begin to affirm that this person's illness is nothing but a distorted thought pattern in form. It is a thing of thought from beginning to end. It has no law to support it, except the law of false belief. He has had enough of it, is through with it, wants no more of it. Let him see himself, or this person, walking up and deliberately taking the disease picture off the wall or the defeat picture, replacing it with one of glorious abundant health and perfection.

Now comes the step where he brings in Power greater than his own. Let him see himself handing this ugly former picture to the Infinite Creative Law to dissolve it and hanging up the new picture of health that it may be condensed into actual experience and form. He then should walk away from it, having completely released it to the Law's hands, thanking the Law for what It is going to do. He should not look back over his shoulder to see whether the Law is working or not. This would be like uprooting the flower to see if it is growing. He should say, "It is done. It is now in the hands of the only agency that can turn thoughts into form."

This is only one way in which the Healing Law may be brought into activity in our behalf. It calls for decisiveness and courage, but it is simple and effective.

That new picture hung upon the wall of mind will stay there unless we hang another in its place. The picture could be replaced by a negative one that says, "I wonder whether the Law is working on it," or "It doesn't seem possible that so simple a prayer could result in healing." Whenever any such doubt pictures try to get hung on the wall, they can be offset by consciously stating, "Of course

63

the Law is working, simply because it is Law. It always works, whether I feel It or not."

If the Wrong Picture Comes, Don't Hang It Up

We can not always prevent negative thoughts entering the mind. But we *can* prevent their getting hung on the mind's wall; this we do by putting into words their exact opposites.

Elsewhere I deal with the tremendous power of the spoken word. It forms a very definite and exact mold into which the Universal Substance flows. If we cannot completely guard our thoughts against these negative invaders, we can always control our words.

Never give utterance to any negative idea. These swarm about us, tenaciously seeking to be hung on the walls, and it is not always possible to prevent their appearance. But we certainly can and must refuse to put them into words. The best treatment to give them is to state their opposites as clearly and confidently as we can. This is exercising our power of choice and initiative, which is the key to the formation of new and constructive mental attitudes.

The choice of friends has much to do with our success in this field. Shun that person who whines and complains, who loves to pounce upon the weaknesses and mistakes of others. Avoid those who dote on their illnesses and whose conversation is chiefly on the morbid happenings in life. Definitely seek out the company of the cheerful person, the one who thinks well of others, who rises above self-pity, whose "conversation is in heaven." We tend to absorb the mental atmosphere of those with whom we associate.

A Basic Prayer for Expectancy of the Good

The following would be a good basic prayer, or prayer treatment, for use in building the expectancy of the Good. It could be used every morning before starting the day's duties; any single paragraph of it could be used, if time were pressing.

This day I move in a bright new world, which is the reflection of my innermost thoughts and beliefs. Consciousness is the only reality; experiences are only the shadow thrown by this reality on the screen of my mind.

This day I consciously and deliberately align myself with the Supreme Consciousness. It always moves in right action; therefore, my affairs this day partake of that all-inclusive principle of right action. I am surrounded by a circle of protection; the Knower within me guides me in all decisions; the Law draws to me those persons, places and things that tend toward my fullest benefit, and I in turn become a blessing to all whom I meet this day. I reject any belief in, or fear of, wrong action.

My body is a temple in which God dwells; all of His methods and activities are those of right action. I welcome every one of these activities and throw myself wide open to them. Nothing destructive can enter or operate within my body this day, for I am deliberately choosing the most constructive molds of thought.

I wish harm or sorrow to none this day; all persons wish me well. My business is indwelt and surrounded by right action. The Knower in me gives me fresh, vital ideas; I meet nice people, make good contacts, close good sales because people like to do business with me.

My spirit sings this day, for I am filled with the consciousness of Life, a Life that is more than physical. I am tuned in to every happy, healthy, successful person this day. Their thoughts travel over invisible paths to me and mine to them. I draw strength from them and they from me. I deliberately disconnect my mental pathways from those who are morbid or ugly, for I am alive only to Truth, Goodness and Beauty.

Nothing negative can find a foothold in me this day. No doubt or fear can attach itself to me. No accidents or mistakes can occur because I walk in a path of right action, both when I am thinking of it and when I am not. I release myself and all my affairs this day to the perfect working of that Perfect Law, which turns these thoughts into things.

This word that I speak I speak not from myself. It is the Word of the great God in me speaking Itself into my experience. This word has All-Power to fulfill itself in my life and affairs this day. It is the most powerful Word in the universe. I release it to the Creative Law of Mind, fully confident that it is even now being fulfilled.

It will be noticed that there is not one word of petition or begging in this prayer. It is simply a statement of belief. It is a declaration, an announcement, a decree that certain things shall be the truth about us this day. Many prayers are only the expression of the panic of the individual; this prayer is an expression of faith. Its answer rests not on the "will-He-or-won't-He" attitude of the person who prays superstitiously; it rests upon the factual statement that the servant does unto us as we believe.

66

There is a familiarizing effect in repetition. Within seven days these statements will not seem farfetched nor brash. The inner level of consciousness will have risen to the point where these seem to be perfectly normal statements to make. But this is only a starter. Henceforth, the curve of consciousness will be upward. The deeper mind will by this time become accustomed to them and will be acting in their coloring, so that the level is found easier to maintain. Better still, we shall have furnished the Creative Law operating in deeper mind with a brand new thought pattern which it will obediently work out as readily as it formerly worked out the negative patterns. As time goes on, this will become the automatic response to life and will seem just as natural as our former attitudes were. From here on, life can never again be the same as it was before. A permanent element is now operating.

Healing Starts Immediately

At this point it might be well to stress the fact that the healing starts the moment the new attitude is taken. Immediately upon receiving its new directions, the Creative Law proceeds to carry them out, whether we observe any change or not. The illness that shows up in November often had its inception in June. From June to November the person was sick although he mistakenly thought he was well. In like manner, the healing that manifests next week or month has already begun, even though the person mistakenly believes himself still to be ill.

This is a tricky point in one's healing. One who is not aware of the instantaneous obedience of the Law may abort the healing by saying, "Well, I did the work but I don't see any change." On the contrary, Job showed his belief by tenaciously declaring, "Though He slay me, yet will I trust in Him." We too must steadily assert our confidence that the Creative Law is at work beneath the surface from the moment we release it to Infinite Mind, "keeping that which we have committed to Him against that day" (of manifestation). The healing that has already started beneath the surface will come to light if we do not waver in our belief, because "without faith it is impossible to please God; for he that cometh to God must believe that He . . . is the rewarder of them that diligently seek Him."

Dr. Alexis Carrel reports that he saw cancer shrink to nothingness while he watched it at the famous shrine of Lourdes. In my activities, I sometimes see instantaneous healing; at other times it is gradual. The rapidity seems to be a matter of individual consciousness.

One should persevere with the work regardless of the forms that show themselves. There is no doubt that an actual Force is in operation the moment we commit ourselves to It. This Force is resistless; no physical force can resist It. It will do Its perfect work. The only force that can block It is our belief. Put your belief on the side of the Infinite and nothing can prevent the perfect work.

Act Brave and You Will Soon Feel Brave

One of the most outstanding salesmen in his field today was once the most dejected. He said, "I don't think I'll ever be a salesman. I'm afraid of my prospects, shrink from interviewing them, and when I do whip up courage to call on them I feel rather relieved when they curtly tell me they are not interested. Then I can make my exit."

68

He went on, "I start out in the morning to make my calls. Then I begin to find excuses. I think, 'It's nine-fifteen. This one will be busy with his mail; he won't want to be bothered. Perhaps that one will not be in yet; maybe I'll go over my sales points for a while.' Perhaps I buy a magazine and read something interesting. By that time I am ready to argue that a prospect will be getting ready to go to lunch. I know these are only excuses. I despise myself for my rationalizing; I try to work up courage, but it doesn't seem to work."

I said, "Feeling follows action rather than precedes it. If you wait until you 'feel' brave you will never feel brave. I suggest that you make a list of more men than you can call on tomorrow. Then *choose* to start promptly at nine and call upon the first one, regardless of the way you feel."

"But I'll probably be so nervous that I won't be able to make a sales talk. I'll make a fool of myself."

"You're making a fool of yourself anyway by sitting in your car doing nothing. I think I can safely guarantee that after the third man has been called on, you'll feel rather eager to tackle the fourth. The control of this whole situation is mental, but we can stimulate the mental by our physical actions. Even if you would find yourself tongue-tied on the first call, you would still be a better man than you are sitting in your car doing nothing. Then *choose* to make the next and the next calls regardless of your feelings. Be willing even to fall flat on your face with fear, but stay with it. *Choosing* to follow what you *know* is correct action will soon make you feel the way you want to feel."

69

That day he sold more than in the previous month. But better still, he had learned one principle of life. He found that the successful man pushes feelings into the background and lives by his coldly considered *choices*. He said that before that day was over he was eager to get to his men and that the problem of courage learned there had made him poised socially as well.

He summed up the whole problem in a few sentences. "Formerly I was sorry for myself, afraid of a turndown, with its resultant awareness of defeat. Now, when arranging my cards for the next day, I feel sorry for these men, because they are going to be sold in spite of the objections they raise. Formerly I went in with the whipped feeling I would have if I were put into the ring with a champion boxer. Now I go in with the feeling that he has only two arms and legs and that if I know my stuff I can take him."

Man's Incredible Power of Choice

Man is the maker of his own bondage; he forges the shackles that hold him in the prison of his false belief. He alone can take the key that frees him. That key is his power of *choice*. Even though his feelings belie the words that he is saying, his freedom lies in that marvelous power to choose. The Book says, "*Choose* you this day whom ye will serve."

The tremendous importance of man's power to *choose* has never been sufficiently stressed. Man usually follows his feelings unaware of the great gift he has in his ability to *choose*. One can *choose* in spite of his feelings, and that which he *chooses* will become the dominant inner pattern of his thought.

Sometimes one has *chosen* to believe that his illnesses were basically unreal, but the pain or distress connected with them has continued to speak louder than his reason. He has thought, "What's the use of trying to delude myself? This distress can not be denied. It is there in spite of what I say about it." And he has given in to his feelings, forgetting that they are much less real than that which his reason speaks.

Our feelings are largely a matter of habit. No recent knowledge has ever displaced William James' finding that "feeling follows action" rather than precedes it.

Man's surface or conscious mind has the functions of reason and selection. His deeper or subconscious mind is the seat of his emotions and feelings. Our feelings about anything are the ultimate result of our *choices* regarding them. Every one of us ultimately comes to feel the way he acts. *We must act the way we believe—or we shall eventually come to believe the way we act.*

Many of us believe ourselves to be the victims of fate or believe that illness is an inescapable nemesis or that some lucky people have it in them to make good, to attract love, to get what they want from life while "we are among the unfortunate ones." Years of this kind of thought set the mold of our thought. Around and in this mold our *feelings* about life develop. These feelings do not make this the truth about us, but a lie believed will act as though it were the truth. Thus, when we determine to *choose* a different thought mold, our feelings rise up and shriek their objections; they have become habituated to accepting our false beliefs as true. So we once more submit weakly

71

to them and are led through the streets on the end of their triumphal rope.

You Can Choose *Confidence and Assurance*

To many it seems too good to be true that we can be free. We have always had experiences of illness, defeat, and loneliness. We think, "Who am I that I should escape the uncertainties of life?" We have not thought far enough; those ropes that hold us are susceptible to one particular solvent, that of the Infinite Healing Presence. Our belief is the one agency in whose presence those ropes of habit dissolve into their native nothingness. Other ropes can be made: the ropes of inner conviction of the good, the beautiful, the true.

Understanding then the nature of our feelings, we make our deliberate *choice* to build a new set of feelings. Since feeling follows action, our first action should be the selection of a *belief* that God intends man to be healthy, happy, and completely integrated within himself. Then we shall as far as possible never give *utterance* to any idea to the contrary. Our human frailty may cause us to slip, perhaps often. But the chief thing is that we have *chosen* to follow what we believe to be a workable hypothesis; the preponderance of our thought and our conversation henceforth will be upon the expectancy of the good and our feelings will gradually come to rally behind this newly cultivated belief.

Fifty years of negative thinking does not take fifty years to reverse. It can come quickly. *Seven days of the new attitudes will have started the pattern.* We shall find ourselves delighted at the considerably brighter attitudes. It will be like living in a brave new world and this is what it is, for it is the world of the Spirit. The third stage is action. We shall begin to act out the part of the person we wish to be. We shall stop commiserating ourselves, or talking about our illnesses. From thought to word to act; this is the divine order.

You Can Choose *a Spiritual Experience*

Under psychological instruction many have gone this far and have been greatly benefited. One may stop on this level if he wishes. He should go one step further, because this additional step will become the keystone of this grand new arch that he desires to build.

He should make it a distinctly spiritual experience. He should go all the way and try to capture the Infinite view of himself.

If his illnesses are only the results of an unreal nightmare, then there must be some center of perfection within him; otherwise, he could never have thought of this perfect freedom. Here is where he makes a big jump. He can say:

All my life I have been looking upon the outer appearance, which is only the hallucination of one in delirium tremens. From this moment I deliberately close my ears to every voice that tells me these delusions are basically real. I *choose* to believe that in God's sight I am unblemished; I now state my belief that the tides of the Infinite Healing Presence are the only reality within me;

73

I walk from now on "in the Light, that lighteth every man that cometh into the world."

By changing the pronoun from first person to third person one can turn the foregoing statement into a very effective prayer treatment for the healing of someone else. This simple statement has been used by thousands of members of my classes for their healing.

Faith Is Action, Not Feeling

One man objected that even if he dared say the words designed to bring about the healing of a loved one he would probably not have "faith" enough to make it work. I told him the following incident to clarify his understanding of faith.

I have been a city dweller much of my life and had never planted anything. Our home in the mountains is in the center of a wild flower district, but there were no flowers immediately near the house. So I bought some packages of wild flower seeds and planted them in a place we could see from the breakfast table. A few days later I said to my wife, "Do you know, I've never planted anything in my life. I don't really believe that those seeds are going to come up."

Her answer was a classic. She said, "Your faith is not necessarily your feeling about those seeds. Your faith consisted in poking those holes in the ground, dropping the seed, and patting the ground. Just wait and see God do

74

the rest." And of course we had a blaze of blue lupins and golden California poppies within the next few weeks.

Faith is not something that we whip up as an interior feeling. St. James said, "You show me your faith without works, and I will show you my faith *by* my works." I evidently had faith that soil, water and sunlight would germinate seeds by the law of their nature regardless of my own feelings. When we pray our faith rests in the soil of the Infinite Ground. We show that faith when we release our thought to it.

When one is praying, he may have no particularly warm feeling that the answer is on the way. He should place his faith on a nonfeeling basis if he can not arouse an appropriate feeling state in regard to it. Let him first believe that the Law of Mind responds to his thought, as I believed the soil would respond. Then even though his feelings proclaim their doubt, let him quietly say, "I would like my feelings to support me in what I am doing, but I believe that Mind responds to me. I am stating the truth about this loved one, and it remains the truth about him *whether or not I feel it to be so.*"

Every advance ever made in man's upward march of civilization has come through deliberate, conscious *choice* against the inertia of feeling. Early man shivered in the wintry cold until one man *chose* to convey fire from a lightning-struck tree into the cave. Man carried burdens on his back until someone *chose* to train animals as beasts of burden. He drove horses until someone *chose* to experiment with steam.

75

The inertia of feeling has kept the great majority content with things as they are. But the advancing, probing minds of a few have always *chosen* to believe that there could be a better way. The history of invention is the triumph of *choice* over feeling. Edison with his light, Ford with his automobile, could have surrendered to feeling a hundred times and quit. But in spite of their feeling of discouragement they *chose* to go on, believing that there was an answer to the seemingly unanswerable problem. We do the *choosing*. The Infinite Creative Law obeys that choice and carries it out.

One is growing rapidly when he can say, "I am believing and knowing in spite of what I feel. My feelings tell me that it's no use trying; then I switch to my power of *choice*, and declare that my faith is in the Law of God's Creative Process rather than in my negative feelings."

For we are told: "Ye shall know the truth, and *the truth* [not your feelings] shall set you free."

*A STORY THAT TEACHES A
NEW LESSON EVERY TIME
YOU READ IT.*

———————

In India, the Spirit of the Plague
passed an old man sitting under a
tree.

Old Man: Where are you going?
Spirit: To Benares, to kill one hundred people.

Later, the old man heard that in
Benares *ten thousand* had died. Then
the Spirit of the Plague passed again
on its return journey.

Old Man: You lied. You said you
would kill one hundred.
Spirit: I killed one hundred. FEAR
killed the rest.

chapter six

Get the World
on *Your* Side

MISS FLINT WAS A BUYER FOR ONE OF THE LARGE DEPART-
ment stores. Modern in every respect, direct in speech,
dressed in a smart business suit, she was a walking model
of efficiency. There were a few hard lines around her eyes
and mouth. One gained the impression that she was always
on guard and that she could take care of herself in competition.

She was bothered by a recurrent colitis. It would
subside and she would think it was cured. But it would
flare up again despite the best efforts of her physician and
she was becoming discouraged.

We shall tell the end before the beginning. I first saw
her six years ago. Today she looks five years younger; she
has had no sign of colitis for five years.

She said, at the time of her first visit to me, "I can't

understand it. My friends have gone to this same doctor. He has done wonders for them. Why not for me?"

"Probably because you have a deeply buried sense of hostility and cross-purposes which they do not have. This could thwart the best efforts of the most skillful physician."

The Parent Thought *of* Hostility

I pointed out that mankind has had much experience of hostility. There have always been quarrels, wars, and competition for the good things of life. For some reason, this deep-seated belief roots itself more firmly in some persons, works beneath the surface, and produces its brood of children. And that's what had happened in Miss Flint's case.

She had come from a laboring-class family. At sixteen she became a department store clerk. Determined to rise, she decided to become a buyer. She paid strict attention to business and became one of their best clerks. She read books on business. She watched carefully the kinds of dresses that sold best, assiduously cultivated the buyers in the various departments, and eventually became a minor assistant to one of them. It took her fourteen grim years to rise to the top and she had held her position for several years. There was no doubt of her capability.

But she had paid the price of success. She had few friends. She had choked off anyone who seemed to threaten her position, had never shared her trade secrets with other buyers. She had secretly determined that she would surpass the buyers in every other department; she would be absolute tops. When a few suggestions would have helped one of them avoid buying something that would be a slow seller, she remained silent, secretly gloating over the fact that their failure would show up her own superiority. She had been filled with a secret rage whenever another buyer achieved a notable success.

I suggested that these attitudes made her somewhat less than a lovable character, to which she replied casually, "That's business."

"Nothing is good business that ruins one's health. This deep-seated belief in hostility and cross-purposes is probably the fundamental cause of your physical condition, and I'm afraid that you will never get rid of the one until you dissolve out the other."

Bacteria Prefer Certain Climates

"Bacteria do not enter our bodies with the intention of destroying us, even though their toxic effects can kill us. They move in for the same reason that we move to certain localities: they like the climate. Those that like other temperatures move into dogs or fish. They bear no hostility toward us. In the proper climate they can carry on the three functions of life—absorbing nutriment, eliminating wastes, and reproducing their kind; in other words, minding their own business.

"Perhaps man's belief in hostility provides the deep seed-bed for many of the diseases of bacterial origin. I agree with the consensus of medical opinion regarding the bacterial origin of many diseases, but I have noticed that when we kill this *parent thought* of hostility and cross-purposes, we rid ourselves of the effects of bacterial illnesses much more quickly."

79

The Infinite Knows No Hostility

"To the person who looks clearly at life there is never any competition. This may sound foolish, especially to the businessman or -woman. But it is so, nevertheless. Since we are trying to line up our thinking with that of the Infinite Thinker, we may lay down one postulate: the Infinite never is aware of any hostile, opposing force. He is never in competition with anything or anyone. We may assume this as a working hypothesis.

"If we can raise our consciousness to this level, we can destroy our false belief in unfair competition and destroy the sense of hostility and cross-purposes that grows out of it.

"Suppose that we start with the assumption that there is an infinite reservoir of all that is good. Since there are more than two billion persons in the world, there must be at least two billion outlets to this reservoir, one for each individual. Each of us can attach himself to an outlet. This outlet becomes inviolably his. No one can enter it or interfere with it. It is his direct pipeline to Infinite Supply.

"If you are the sort of person who thinks in pictures you can picture this pipe as being attached to the Infinite Reservoir at one end and attached to the top of your head at the other. It does not matter whether this is the actual way it is attached or not. You are trying to build a certain belief; the result is more important than the means."

"But," objected Miss Flint, "someone else might want what *I* have!"

"Many people think they want what others have. They plot, scheme, and work to push someone aside so that they may inherit what he has gained. But your position is unassailable, because only that can come to you which you believe.

"You alone can wrench the connecting pipe loose by your lack of faith and by your practice of the belief in competition. It may be in the minds of millions; if it is not in you it can not happen to you."

The Right of Consciousness

"If the envious person could see clearly he would know that I have gained my good by what Emerson calls *the right of consciousness*. No other person really wants what I have; he wants a *similar* experience. He can have it when he goes after it in the truly scientific way. If he develops my type of consciousness he will receive the kind of experience that I have received.

"This line of reasoning removes all envy and jealousy from our hearts. We shall never again hold a suppressed rage toward a competitor who is succeeding. If he outpaces us we shall look within ourselves for the cause of our failure. We will 'rejoice with them that rejoice' in their success. We will use their success as a stimulant to our faith, knowing that it will be done unto us as we believe."

Much more was said. At first Miss Flint squirmed, but she did not evade. Life had already taught her that one must stand up and face unpleasant facts. She faced them. She set out with businesslike efficiency to change her thoughts. Her physical trouble disappeared. During the next few months it flared up occasionally, but within half a year it left forever, as she perfected the change in her innermost thinking.

Perhaps any illness of bacterial origin could be handled in this way. I have seen hundreds cleared up. History reports many instances in which the self-sacrificing person, filled with a heart of love, has moved untouched among people stricken with typhus and other highly contagious diseases. Who will deny that the absence of any harboring of hostility might have been its own prophylaxis?

In an earlier chapter we dealt with the *parent thought* of irritation and its baby, Mr. Bludgin's ulcer. Miss Flint's colitis actually is a disease of irritation. The Greek ending *-itis* is used to denote inflammation or irritation. Why is it that we attribute her trouble to the *parent thought* of hostility?

The fact is that some of us entertain several of the *parent thoughts*. They intermingle in us so that it is difficult to separate them. But it is certain that he who is dominated by the *parent thought* of hostility is bound to be *irritated* by the success of another, or by the efforts of another to dislodge him. Man is a complicated being. Our minds are deeper than we think and far more complex in their interweavings.

One of my medical friends once asked, "How do you account for the fact that man suffered from bacterial diseases long before he knew of bacteria?" The obvious reply was that one need not think of a *condition* in order to suffer it; nor need he know any of the processes by which he suffers any illness.

The *parent thought* believed will produce its own children in its own time. The fact that we have the emotion is evidence that we have the underlying belief. Animals have emotions such as rage and fear. Their illnesses are the result of these for the most part; illnesses are not God's punishment for sin; they are the inescapable consequences of destructive thought.

Long before man appeared on the earth, the prehistoric animals developed bone tumors and other diseases, as their fossils reveal. Illness is the outgrowth of distorted emotions. Never a punishment, it is an automatic effect. Fortunately, man has the type of mind that can uncover this fact and alter his beliefs to conform to it.

Many a wife has lost her husband to a rival; brides have been left at the altar; salesmen have lost good accounts; persons have lost their jobs through what they have thought to be double-crossing by others. It was the automatic working out of their *parent thought* of competition, hostility, and cross-purposes.

"My Own Shall Come to Me"

Someone might ask, "But is there not real competition where two persons are in love with the same man or woman, where two men want the same job, or two persons want the same house?"

Even here they are not necessarily in competition. We fall in love with a type rather than with a particular person, place, or thing. Even he who is deliriously happy in his marriage would have been as enthralled with the loved one if he had lived in South Africa and had fallen in love with a different person.

He would never have known of the existence of the present spouse. Even in this country he could have married any one of ten thousand others and have been just as happy. But each of those ten thousand would have borne the same qualities that evoked his love for this one. She might have differed in height, coloring, or other details. But somewhere there would have been the hidden tie that binds together hearts of a certain type.

It is for this reason that one need never be hopelessly cast down when he has lost love. That one is unconsciously speaking untruth who says, "She is the only person I have ever loved. I could never love again." Many widowed or jilted persons have found sublime joy with a second mate.

Once we catch the idea that everything we want from life is typed we find it easier to divest ourselves of the false belief in competition, hostility, and cross-purposes. One can quite strongly admire another, want him, be "in love" with him. However, under our laws two cannot have him at the same time. Wise then is that one who approaches the great surrounding Infinite Mind with some such prayer treatment as the following: (For clarity I am using the feminine gender.)

This is the type of man with whom I could be supremely happy. Whatever it is in him that awakens this response in me, it is something peculiar to our particular types.

There are women who would be quite unresponsive to this type of man, but I respond, therefore my mind and his are united at some point. I do not need to work on him as an individual to make him want me. He either responds equally to what I am or he does not. If not, I have no right to my happiness if it would not bring him equal happiness. But I am quietly *knowing* within myself that a man of this type is being drawn to me. "My own shall come to me." I do not have to fight anyone else who wants him; I do not need to throw obstacles in her way, nor to belittle her to him. My attraction for him will draw to me either him or someone else who is of the type.

People coming into this system of thought sometimes ask, "I have fallen in love with a certain man; how can I use this principle to make him fall in love with me?" Such a use of the law is in the nature of hypnotism or black magic. It is an invasion of the man's personality. We have no right to work on anyone else to make him do anything of the sort. Working as in the previous paragraph will draw to us either him or another like him.

The same applies to a particular job, the buying of a home, or the sale of property to a certain prospect. These things are not done in a compulsive way. It is not necessary. When the general principle is applied, the particular way always opens within the limits of right action. The trouble is that we are impatient and in our childishness we "want what we want when we want it." Often we find that what we get in this way is not what we really wanted.

Being Comes before Getting

Unbelievers have often scoffed at the ridiculousness of two nations each praying to the same God to give them victory in war, or of two boxers "crossing themselves" in prayer as they start each round. They who understand the creative principle approach this seeming dilemma from a different angle, as I shall illustrate.

Some time ago our former church soloist entered the Atwater-Kent vocal competition, along with fifteen hundred other hopefuls. In order to help a talented young man and to show our congregation how such situations are handled, I asked them to pray for him in the following way: We would not ask God to make him the winner; we would pray by inducing within ourselves the conviction that his bearing would be appropriate; that his tones would be pure and true; that his technique would be correct; that the accent in his foreign language songs would be true; and, above all, that he would be quietly assured within himself that he would give the very best performance of which he was capable.

Within ourselves we likewise would endeavor to hold steady in emergencies, cool under fire, peaceful under any irritation that might arise in our own lives. Thus our own thought atmosphere would not deny the words that we were speaking for him in these prayers. It will be noticed that we were praying for him to *be* something rather than to *get* something.

For months eliminations were held. Finally twelve singers were left in the semifinals. Six of these survived into the finals which were to be held in Los Angeles and broadcast on the radio. Our man was among them. We sat quietly at the radio that night. I am sure that he will not feel hurt if I say that I believe there were at least two out of the six who had slightly better voices. Yet when the awards were made, Albert Wilcox was the winner, receiving the gold medal and a substantial cash award. He has since gone into well-paid professional work.

It is not always the most highly endowed who gain life's prizes. The proper state of mind must be added to the natural gift. It is the person in his entirety who rises or falls. "What is mine shall surely come to me *by the right of consciousness*."

It might be objected that this is a form of self-hypnosis, in which we delude ourselves into believing something that is not so. Quite the opposite! Man has so long believed himself a worm of the dust, conceived in sin and born in iniquity, under the condemnation of an outraged God, that he has lost sight of the fact that he is an aspiring upward-looking being; that far from being under the censure of a disapproving God he is being sought as the partner and co-worker with God.

Since many have repeatedly failed while few have succeeded, the man on the street has come to echo the words of Job's comforter, "Man is born to trouble as the sparks fly upward." Thus life seems to agree with the pessimist that man is normal when failing and unhappy.

We disagree! Any idea held steadily in mind is bound to come forth in experience. Start a child out by allowing him to hear his parents bemoan the fact that life is hard. Let the conversation in the home and the headlines in the papers occupy themselves with the tragedies of life, of Aunt Emma's illness, Joe Jones' death, and the arrest of the neighbor boy for stealing a car. Let radio and television talk of man's ills and sell nostrums to make the misery less. Let the newspapers headline the terrible crashes and brutal murders, and the child is conditioned to believe that he is lucky if he survives the horrible dangers of this world. Thus his mind is twisted by a picture impressed upon it.

Is it any wonder then that many have an acceptance of tragedy and defeat by the time they are twenty? Only a sturdy few break through and demand that life shall come to their terms. These are they who succeed.

The negative stories may be a recital of "facts." All that they depict may be true. But we must go further back. *Why* is it true? Because the other side has never been adequately presented. Illness, poverty, wars, and exploitation of the weaker by the stronger are secondary facts; they are effects. They arise out of the primary fact that man has believed himself subject to the vicissitudes of life. He should have been taught that he is master of life.

Man Is Made for Winning

The very first promise in the Bible is that man shall subdue and have dominion over "the earth." But man's earth nature has been allowed to assume the dominance. It is an impostor, a squatter on divine territory. Man's spirit has primary rights and irresistible powers; he has allowed himself to be bulldozed or tricked out of them.

It cannot be repeated too often that when Jesus urged men to repent, He never intended that they should grovel before God. He meant that they should completely change their approach to life. He wanted them to see their God-given destiny to rise superior to everything of earth. In the only prayer He taught, He mentioned sin only once, when He said, "Forgive us our debts [sins] as we forgive our debtors." Even this has been translated, "*Thou forgivest* us our debts as we forgive our debtors," changing it from a petition into a statement of fact. It is a statement of the absence in us of a belief in hostility.

Words without Consciousness Go without Results

When man affirms his statement of belief he sets in motion a tremendous current of power. When he can make his declaration without any mental reservations, he is nearing the answer to prayer. But a word of warning is necessary concerning "affirmations."

An affirmation is a statement of belief that embodies some particular truth. Written usually by a spiritually minded person, it is sometimes picked up by a follower and repeated as a talisman. Unless this second person catches the consciousness of the writer, he will be repeating words only. This is superstition.

A statement of spiritual truth is potent only when the inner heart consciousness and the outer words coincide with each other. But when the person thus thoughtfully prays with both surface and deeper mind, he comes into a position of tremendous power, and a specific interaction of his mind and God's mind takes place.

This interaction of human and divine is the secret of man's mastery of life, of the healing of the body, and of the manifestation of the Good in all his affairs. It has a startling effect upon a person when first he sees it, but it contains the secret of his "subduing the earth and having dominion over it."

It is pitiful to hear persons parroting beautifully conceived phrases without the slightest conception of their inner meaning and significance. They seem to cling to the notion that there is some magic in the words themselves. The Lord's Prayer is a series of statements of rare spiritual consciousness. It must make the angels weep to hear it as it is sometimes unthinkingly raced through in a church service. David had the perception to know the danger of this. He prayed, "Let the words of my mouth *and* the meditation of my heart be acceptable in Thy sight, O Lord."

Problem of the Timid Person

The *parent thought* of hostility does not always show itself as plainly as in Miss Flint. Hostility often masks itself. Shy people, timid salesmen, "wallflowers," and all who withdraw from contacts with people are to be suspected of entertaining this *parent thought* of hostility. It is the chief cause of the inferiority complex. A totally false picture of himself and others causes the timid person to draw apart from others, inwardly if not outwardly. He is revealing his unconscious hostility.

The timid person is timid because of an unconscious feeling that others are against him. He is silent in company, fearing that he does not have "the gift of gab" and that others will criticize him behind his back for his insipid contribution to the discussion.

A salesman who shrank from making calls, and who as a consequence was not selling anything, was asked, "Just *what* is it you are afraid of in your prospects?"

"I don't know. I'm just afraid, that's all."

"But fear always has a specific object. There's no such thing as just being afraid of nothing. Are you afraid that he will call the police and have you arrested? Or that he will throw you out physically? Or that he will hit you with a baseball bat?"

He laughed. "Of course not. Such things would be ridiculous."

He was brought to the point where he could see that he had built up an unconscious hostility toward his prospects, based upon his belief that they would be hostile to his presentation of his product, which was an excellent home study course in business law put out by a reputable organization.

He came to see that, although not all businessmen would want or need this service, the great majority of his specially selected prospects would find it of tremendous value. He placed himself mentally in their shoes, asked himself exactly where and in what way this would be of benefit. He pictured the demands on a man for his time and knew that most men don't like a salesman taking that time, especially when they have not been brought to see the great value of the item being sold. But he knew that if a man could be brought to see this service as the salesman saw it, he would happily grant the time to have it explained.

Now he ceased seeing himself as an unwelcome nuisance. He saw himself as a benefactor. One does not hold feelings of hostility toward a benefactor, nor does the benefactor entertain feelings of a similar nature. Here then is friend meeting friend.

Of his own accord the salesman thought of cultivating the feeling: "This man is my friend and I am his. He likes me and I like him. When he is using our service he will always think gratefully of the fact that I brought it to his attention. He needs it, wants it, buys it."

We have already brought out the fact that hostility

is separation while love is unity. With this man we used the term *good will* or *well-wishing* instead of *love*—the former being more acceptable to a salesman.

The net result was that his changed inner expectation brought him much easier contacts. He said that where previously he had been met with a curt "Well, what's on your mind? I'm pretty busy," he would now often be met with a friendly "What can I do for you?"

His own inner tension lifted, he could make a much better presentation in shorter time, and in many instances the sale was closed on the first call.

This salesman was slightly embarrassed when I told him one day that now he was becoming godly in his thinking. But it was the truth. The Infinite is never occupied with thoughts of hostility on the part of anyone toward Him and certainly never entertains feelings of hostility toward others. As the man took on more of the divine attitude he was thinking God's thoughts after Him in a nonreligious manner; he was becoming Godlike.

The Center of Our Affections Must Be Outside Ourselves

One of the greatest helps in overcoming the inferiority complex is the cultivation of a genuine good will. We are told that "love is the fulfilling of the Law." He who is filled with feelings of inferiority has placed himself at the center of his own affections. His thought is continually upon himself, the impression he is making, the opinion others hold of him, their possible criticisms, the possibility of their hurting him. Love is the placing of another at the center.

"Love thinketh no evil." "Perfect love casteth out

fear." These are not only religious truths. They are psychological principles. When one shifts the center of his attention from himself and develops a central interest in others, he begins to free himself from his timidities. When he moves toward the expectation of a warm welcome from others and cultivates a feeling of sincere good will toward others, he moves rapidly toward freedom from his self-imposed prison. When he is willing that they laugh at him if they want to, he has moved high on that road. The poet offered a way of escape when he said, "Be self forgot in serving others' need."

COMPETITION

becomes

an opportunity for

ACCOMPLISHMENT

when you

overcome the parent thought of

HOSTILITY

and think of the world

as a

FRIENDLY PLACE

in which there is enough to satisfy all.

chapter seven

Get Out of Your Way

MISS SADD WAS BEAUTIFUL EVEN IN TEARS. IT WAS THE SAME old story, seen often in Hollywood. She had won a beauty contest in her home town and had started out to take Hollywood by storm. In spite of her undeniable attractiveness she had been turned down by every studio she had called on. She had taken a job as a waitress. Now she was in trouble. When she had pleaded with the man to marry her, he had laughed in her face and told her, "Babes as good-looking as you are a dime a dozen out here."

She wanted to know why all her life she had been able to bring things up to a certain point, but had never been able to complete them. She said, "From the time I was a child, things have never come easy for me. Everything I've ever wanted has come only after long postponements or after terrific struggle. The only thing that came

95

quickly was my selection in the contest and that came only after horrible squabbling among the contestants, their parents, and friends. The town was split into factions over it. But I've never been able to get what I wanted when I wanted it."

The *parent thought* in this case is one that is very prevalent. It is the same one that allows the salesman to bring his prospect up to a certain point but kills the deal before it can be closed. It keeps people from selling property; many look but no one buys. Girls fail to receive proposals of marriage; some never even get a date. It operates also very decidedly in the body. Coronary occlusion, stoppages, irregularities of one sort or another all seem to stem from this underlying parent thought of *obstruction and delay*. Yet, like all of the others, it can be dissolved when approached intelligently.

God Is Never Blocked

The belief in obstruction and delay is something entirely foreign to God's thinking. As we have said previously, we can gain some idea of the divine thinking by watching the evidences of it in the universe around us.

"The heavens declare the glory of God"; they declare the nature of God also. We deduce that there is nothing of obstruction and delay in the Infinite thought because "the stars come nightly to the sky," the seasons roll around with ceaseless regularity, the seed germinates in plant and animal, and offspring come forth practically to the minute. Where events take longer than man would wish, as in the slower movements of nature, this seems to be the regular schedule for that particular type of event; therefore, it is no evidence of delay. But where anything is unduly delayed in man's affairs, he can refuse to accept it and do something definite to hurry it up.

In many instances, we have been able to trace the inception of this belief back into the early days of childhood. In this instance, the little girl had been shopping one day with her mother; she had fallen in love with a shiny tricycle and had begged for it. Her mother had said, "I'll get it for you for Christmas." The child was delighted, not knowing that Christmas was still three months distant. Every few days she would ask for the tricycle. "But when will Christmas be, Mummy?" "Not long now," her mother always answered. Instead of keeping the child's spirits up, this answer had the effect of depressing her, and may have laid the foundation for her belief in obstruction and delay.

Her mother started once to make for her what Miss Sadd called "a darling dress," but other duties kept her from working steadily on it. Then her mother went to the hospital to have another baby and was gone almost two weeks, an interminable time for the eager child who every day fingered the partly finished dress. To an adult this might seem foolish, but we we must remember that we are dealing with the eager three-year-old to whose time schedule "a day is as a thousand years." In fact, all of our complexes and fears are foolish, but we start taking them on during those childhood days of limited reason when desire and other emotions are dominant.

How Parent Thoughts Grow

The *parent thought* accepted becomes a magnet to attract to itself similar thoughts. It grows in strength by feeding upon similar experiences, the memories of which fall into the deeper levels of mind and gravitate to the *parent thought* until a considerable history of frustration and delay has formed—or irritation, hostility, or any of the others. This in turn leads into an unconscious expectation that it is no use setting one's heart too strongly upon anything since we shall probably be hindered from getting it. Thus a *belief* in obstruction and delay is built, which lies deep within even when we imagine we do not have anything of the sort.

Often people have countered by saying, "But I did *not* have that belief. I wanted this or that and felt sure that I was going to get it." Which brings us back to the fact that the mind is tricky and elusive, concealing many of its strongest streams of thought far beneath the surface.

Miss Sadd's religious training had consisted in memorizing certain Bible verses in Sunday School. But she was quite vague about the meaning of most of them. I asked if there were any particular verses she remembered. She said, "I always liked that one about the Vine and the branches, because I liked grapes so much."

"That's as good a place as any to start," I said. Then I explained that if a vine could talk, it would probably say that it liked grapes also; that it earnestly desired grapes. This is not so far-fetched since everything in the universe seems to want to fulfill its nature, and it is the nature of the vine to bear grapes. Therefore, it puts out buds, indicating that it is getting ready for grapes.

Dare to Expect the Best

The first thing Miss Sadd had to build was an expectancy of results. She wanted marriage. But she pointed out that no one wanted to marry someone in her condition. I quoted that part of the vine passage which said, "If ye abide in me and my words abide in you, ye shall ask *what ye will* and it will be done unto you." The natural tendency of most of us is to think of all the reasons why our desires can *not* come into fulfillment; the Infinite thinks of all the reasons why His desire *can* come forth. He does not believe in frustration and delay. Miss Sadd said that she had no right to talk of abiding in the Vine because she had sinned. I pointed out that another girl once made a similar mistake and that Jesus had said, "Neither do I condemn thee. Go and sin no more."

Miss Sadd learned that abiding in the Vine is nothing mysterious. It simply means trying to think God's type of thoughts after Him. The need for brevity compels us to compress the story, but this girl caught the idea rapidly. We worked on the idea that the fulfillment of life could come now, soon, in short time; that nothing in the universe forbade it; that life is neutral toward us, neither refusing us nor bringing to us without our consent, but always responding to our inward convictions when we definitely assume the leadershp.

Her baby was born three months later. The taxi driver who drove her to her apartment from the hospital was a young veteran whose application was in for the job of motorcycle policeman. He talked about himself as he drove, telling how glad he was that she was well, since his own wife had died in childbirth two years before. He said his two-year-old boy was always asking for a sister and he asked if her husband would object if he brought the little fellow around to see the baby sometime. She said she had no husband but would be glad to show the baby to the boy. One need not stretch the imagination to foresee that within six months she had a police officer for a husband and the boy had his little sister.

Heart Disease Is Heartache

Dr. Flanders Dunbar has shown that the type of person who suffers coronary occlusion is a conscientious, hard-working man with a strong sense of responsibility toward his family, and with a consuming ambition to rise to the top in his field. This kind of person naturally meets with much obstruction on the way to the top. He wants rapid promotion or growth; he chafes at the apparent delay in reaching his goals. The outsider sees him from the outside and is impressed with the way he gets what he goes after. But he, knowing himself from within, knows that his whole life is a series of obstructions to be overcome, a series of delays to be accelerated. This type never makes as rapid progress as he desires.

Mr. Putsch was such a man. In his early forties he was third man from the top in a giant corporation. It looked as if he would soon go all the way, but a heart attack laid him aside. In bed for two months, he came to see me on the recommendation of another man who had been helped in a similar situation. Gentle-spoken, he would never be picked out as one of the most productive executives, but he was a man of prodigious inner force.

He agreed that his whole life had seemed to be one of obstruction and delay. He said, "I need forty-eight hours in every day to do all that I see to be done."

It developed that his method of handling obstruction and delay was, as he put it, to "turn on the steam." He battled, wrestled, struggled with baffling situations until he had beaten them to the ground.

I pointed out to Mr. Putsch that his firm *belief* in obstructions gave them most of their reality. The obstructions he met were chiefly beliefs that he had turned into things. Then he was compelled to fight these things that he himself had created.

Is It a Belief or Actuality?

I liked the way he fought back. He said, quietly but very intently, "Now listen! I have men standing around idle at this moment because a train wreck a thousand miles away is keeping raw materials from the plant. You may call that a belief. I call it an actuality."

We Get What We Expect

"So do I! But the actualities grow out of beliefs; in fact they *are* the belief having taken form. All of your life went into that train wreck. All your previous system of beliefs was showing itself in many of the incidents you have told me of. Cause is often quite remote from effect as we see it, but cause and effect are inseparably linked. Not any single thought, but your general system of thought, finds its effects in obstructions over and over; another man would not run into so many difficulties.

"Bring yourself to the place where you do not see obstructions and delay threatening every move you make. Get into that frame of mind where you believe that you have a Silent Partner who agrees with you that there is a clear road ahead. He sees no obstructions. You are of His nature, and you have no right to encounter obstructions. Learn how to expect the good to happen. Every morning when you wake, deliberately ask yourself, 'I wonder what good things will happen today, what good contacts I shall make, what good deals will be closed, what good work will be done at the plant.' Cultivate the expectancy of the good rather than of trouble. Don't tell yourself that you are only kidding yourself when you say this. Saying the opposite is kidding yourself because the Infinite sees no obstruction; don't stress the fact that business is full of disappointments and delays. Even if this is true, you only magnify it by holding it at the focus of your attention.

"Your thoughts may not have precipitated that train wreck. But men who have adopted this method of cultivating the expectancy of the good have told me that their materials have been rerouted from the train upon which they were slated to go, thus avoiding a wreck or a washout somewhere, or their shipments have been shipped a day earlier, or some disposition has been made of them that brings them through on time and in good order. Without their even thinking about danger, they have missed a plane or taken a different one; one man was put off a plane to make room for a V.I.P. during the war and was writing a scorching letter about it to the authorities when word came that the plane had crashed.

"Suppose you try another tack. I have found that seven days is usually sufficient to test out *parent thoughts*. Will you take these days quietly at home, since you are not working, and review what you can see in the universe bearing out that the Superintending Intelligence operates without delay and obstruction?"

You Can See Yourself in the Universal

"Take everything, however small, that bears out my thesis. Act as if you really *want* to believe, without being blindly credulous.

"But be sure to think *yourself* into the happenings that you observe. The least imaginative scientist sees the resistless tides of force that I am asking you to see—but he sees it only as the working of 'natural law.' He sees something remote, something with which he is not personally connected. You must see *yourself* as part of the universe. For precisely the same law that operates the universe must be ready to operate in one of its parts.

"In a friendly way think of God as trying to think His thoughts through you. If you wish, you can tell Him that you are willing that He should do so. Then for your own edification say quietly, 'Infinite God thinks through me with the same lack of frustration and delay that I see in His thinking through the lesser fragments of the universe.' That is all you need at the present time."

He said, "Now that makes sense. I'll try it." The first thing he saw as he went to his car was a cardboard carton lying in the center of the street. A passing car crushed it. The car also ran over a shaft of sunlight that lay across the pavement. But the sunlight, far from being crushed, mounted the car and then resumed its place on the pavement.

This was a trifling incident, but Mr. Putsch thought, "The Mind that controls that sunlight is in me right now. So I rise above whatever would crush me. I am superior to everything that menaces me, my peace of mind, my success, my company, or my home and children."

He thought of the silent pull of gravitation that held his heavy car to the road without strain or struggle. He saw the moon that night and thought of the effortless pull that makes it circle the earth every twenty-nine days, and he reflected that the moon had circled for a billion years without ever being late. He went on to think of the resistless pull of the moon on the tides. From this viewpoint it was easy to see himself in partnership with an Impulse that had never been successfully obstructed.

One day he sat convalescing in his yard. He gave his attention to a rosebud. Within a few hours, he saw it slowly bloom into a rose, easily, effortlessly, without seeming to overcome any obstruction.

Mr. Putsch made himself part of all these phenomena. He knew that they were all expressions of "a Mathematical Thinker thinking mathematically," as astrophysicist Sir James Jeans has put it. He began to find a new warm feeling toward God creeping in. Heretofore, he had thought of Him with decided reluctance and a certain feeling of strangeness, if not of fear. But now he found himself feeling a kind of kinship with the Infinite, a new friendliness such as he entertained toward his fellow executives who helped him work out problems.

When one's false beliefs are healed, the whole man is healed. Several years have passed and Mr. Putsch has no coronary trouble today. Incidentally, he has become active in his church.

It is a pity that the approach to God has been made to seem chiefly a thing of creed and otherworldliness, when it is really a practical partnership.

EXPECT THE BEST
and you'll get it!

EXPECT THE WORST
Delay

Frustration

Obstruction

or whatever is blocking your happiness *and that's what you'll get!*

The choice is yours. Why not dare to expect the best and let the Creative Process silently clear away the debris of a disordered life?

~~~~~~~~~~~~~~~~~~~~~~~~~~~~~~~~~~~~~~

chapter eight

Sailing Through

~~~~~~~~~~~~~~~~~~~~~~~~~~~~~~~~~~~~~~

MRS. WEAKLEY WAS PARALYZED ALONG ONE SIDE AS THE result of a stroke. She came to Long Beach, California, with a nurse who helped her in and out of a wheelchair. Hearing of my lectures in that city, she asked me to call upon her in the Robinson Hotel where she was staying. She explained that she had suffered from this condition for several years and that her sons had taken her to the best neurologists, all of whom said she would never walk again.

During the discussion it developed that she had been widowed and that certain experiences in her life had seemed so devastating that, in her own words, "I didn't know how I could face them."

I called upon her twice, explained our theory of the *parent thoughts* and prayed with her.

On my third visit, her nurse said as I entered, "Mrs. Weakley has a new trick she wants to show you." At that, the woman got out of bed and remained standing for a few minutes without the support of the nurse. She said, "A few days ago I did this for the first time since my stroke."

The next week she said, "I have another new trick for you." She repeated what she had previously done, then limped around the bed without assistance, except to touch it occasionally, then around the room, taking somewhat halting steps and reaching out to maintain her balance by touching various articles of furniture.

Spiritual Healing Gives Spiritual Independence

I had not asked her to walk. I never tell someone, "Now you are well, rise and walk." Nor do I tell the diabetic to eat sugar, nor the person with ulcer to eat celery and string beans or other fibrous food. My work with people does not go into medical practice; it consists of explaining the principle, praying with them and leaving them to work out their own salvation. Once the principle is understood anyone can use it. Thus, they are not made dependent upon me; they become spiritually self-sufficient. These "tricks" Mrs. Weakley was learning were of her own volition entirely.

This went on for a couple of months and she was getting ready to leave again for her midwestern home. She still walked with a limp, but had made remarkable progress. A few days before she was to leave, her son wired that he would be in California in a few days and would run down to Long Beach for a few hours with her.

Learning the exact time of his arrival, Mrs. Weakley with her nurse awaited him in a remote corner of the lobby. Her son entered, walked to the desk and asked for her. At this, the two ladies rose and walked slowly toward him. Her son turned and saw her without wheelchair, crutch, or other visible support; his eyes widened with fear; he said frantically, "Mother, take care," and rushed to her support. She waved him away and said, "Let's go up to the room and talk."

"But, Mother, I just can't believe my eyes," he said. "Whatever have you been doing? What treatment have you had?"

"I'm afraid you won't approve. I've received these results through prayer," she said.

To which he replied, "I wouldn't care if you had got them through the Devil himself, just as long as I see you walk."

The Parent Thought *of* Overload *at Work*

Mrs. Weakley's cure came when she rid herself of the *parent thought* of *overload*. Remember that her own phrase for her troubles was "I didn't know how I could face them." She saw herself as inadequate, in danger of being submerged by life's experiences.

The feeling of overload is not uncommon among humans. Many people in this lonely, desperate state of mind, feeling themselves all alone in the universe, stepchildren of Fate, respond with some such expression of despair as "I can't go through with it," or "This is more than I can bear."

William Henley must have been threatened with this

state of mind when one of his feet had been amputated and he was threatened with loss of the other. In response, however, he wrote, "Under the bludgeonings of chance my head is bloody but unbowed." His poem *Invictus* has become the inspiration for many who are threatened with the mother thought of overload.

The first thing Mrs. Weakley had to be brought to see was this: The body is continually swept by the stream of thought emerging from the brain. In the process, the *brain* consciousness becomes the *cell* consciousness. Since the principal quality of matter is inertia, it follows that the body of itself cannot originate a disease.

This fact is important for the person who would heal himself. It shifts the deciding factor in his recovery away from the uncertain actions of the body to the more certain procedures that he can originate in his mind. Instead of feeling insecure and helpless in the grip of a body that will not behave, he comes to see that the body is his servant. He realizes that he can start to reform his inner thought patterns, thus presenting the cells with thoughts of their perfect structure and function.

The person now sees the true picture of himself, inflicting illness upon a body that does not want it. Health is natural, sickness unnatural. If the cells could speak they would say, "Please, you up there, will you change what you're sending down here because we're quite uncomfortable. We'll gladly cooperate if you will."

It must be reiterated that the body does not break down of its own volition. A muscle or a nerve does not decide that it will refuse to function. It is *compelled* to

cease by the thinker in the body, who often is quite ignorant of the fact that he is imposing limitation on the body.

The Universe Is Never Overloaded

It is a fundamental that every structure in the universe
is built to sustain its own load. The body is no exception
to this law.

A speaker at the convention of the American Heart
Association said recently that the fear of dropping dead is
more dangerous than the heart condition from which the
patient suffers. There are tremendous reserves built into
the heart. It will continue to pump and thump even when
badly out of order, as if it were trying to stay on the job
in spite of the bad mental treatment it gets.

The body in general is built to endure far more strain
than we ordinarily put upon it. There is a tremendous
margin of stress built into it. Any one of the paired organs
such as kidneys and lungs will carry the organism along
nicely if the other is destroyed. The survivor enlarges to
do the work of its mate as well as its own.

Authorities tell us that we could lose three-fourths of
the liver; the remaining tissue would still keep us going.
With four-fifths of the thyroid gone, life can continue sat-
isfactorily. Nine-tenths of the adrenal glands could disappear without endangering the life function. Many of the
organs have ten to fifteen times their normal capacity built
into them. Man worries too much over the body. If it
could think independently it might worry over this timid
creature who inhabits and dominates it.

Mrs. Weakley had this tremendous margin of safety

in her muscles and nerves, but she depleted it by the draining away of her courage and hope. Man has been told, "When thou passest through the deep waters, I will be with thee," and "There hath no testing fallen upon thee that thou canst not bear; for God will not allow you to be tested without any way of escape." These are God's guarantees against overload. But man forgets these when the storms of life rage around him. He becomes panicky. Visions of tragedy are constantly before his eyes. He sees himself overwhelmed, sinking, destroyed. His total picture is "I'll never be able to go through this." It's a complete picture of overload.

The body knows nothing of overload. Its brave resourcefulness is shown in the way it quickly adapts to excessive strains or deprivation of its parts. Block or sever a blood vessel; it will quickly start to build new channels to bypass the blockage. But day after day, perhaps month after month, it is presented with this mental picture of inadequacy by one whose false belief in overload is persistent.

The time comes when the body must succumb to the steady pressure of the overload thought. It can no longer maintain its defenses; these slowly—sometimes quickly—disintegrate. Then man, the thoughtless thinker, wonders why he should be made to suffer, quite innocent of the fact that he himself has unwittingly brought it about.

Life Cannot Break Us Down

Overload is an ungodly thought. The Infinite God knows nothing of overload and has no fear of it. The person who fears that he will be overwhelmed by life, resigning himself to illness because it is "the will of God," is ungodly.

We start with the logical assumption, "like Father, like son." Man must cultivate the attitudes toward life that God has. If he is a Bible follower, he can do it through the promises with which that wonderful Book is loaded. Or he can do it through reading God's second book, Nature. For Infinite Intelligence reveals itself to different persons in different ways.

Johann Kepler said, turning from his study of the movements of the celestial bodies, "Oh God, I am thinking Thy thoughts after Thee."

The principal requirement for healing is that man establish a contact with something greater than himself. This has always been the secret of power. Alcoholics Anonymous have proved it to be the secret of freedom from excessive drinking. They do not attempt to define God nor to bind a man to any particular system of religious belief, for men in all religious systems have found God through different pathways. The important thing for the individual is that he establish the kind of contact that fits in with his type of mind and religious background.

When one knows that there is something within him that is greater than anything that can ever confront him, life can never break him down. He can endure anything, undergo any trials and come through successfully. I learned this forty years ago. It not only led to my healing; it gave me an illuminating concept of life that has taken me over some rough places throughout the ensuing years.

The picture of overload is a lie. But this lie believed will act to confirm itself. It will produce destructive effects in business affairs and in the body. These offspring of the *parent thought* will partake of its characteristics, and one may expect anything from nervous breakdowns to bankruptcy.

On the other hand, "the truth shall set us free." The truth is that man has the right to manifest in himself the conditions that mirror God's perfection. The seeds of perfection are within man; his business is to allow them to come into fruition.

"Be ye perfect as your Father in heaven is perfect." This command has always been a stumbling-block to struggling man. He has thought that God is asking the impossible of him. But we must place this problem first in the world of thought. "*Think* of yourself as perfect, as your Father in heaven thinks of Himself (and of you as His manifestation) as perfect."

None of us ever achieves perfection here, but raising our sights to the immaculate perfection of the Father will free us from the effects of a belief in overload.

God Thinks His Adequacy through Us

Here is a prayer treatment that many have found effective:

> I know that my body was created as a perfect instrument for all of God's adequacy. Every nerve and muscle of the body knows this. It is its nature faithfully to perform every function easily and competently.
>
> Infinite God has never seen anything that could resist His movement. He has never had the slightest qualm concerning His ability to carry the load of the entire universe. Every star and planet is manipulated easily and effortlessly

in its march through space. Staggeringly heavy, they are as puff balls in His powerful hands.

His mind is my mind. His qualities are mine. His effortless approach to burdens is mine also. He is my strength, because He thinks through my thoughts. Nothing could possibly overload me or break me down, for it then would be overloading the Father in heaven. This is not possible.

I face the darkest moment of life with His courage. There is no desire in me to shrink or to run away from any load I have to carry. Even the heaviest trial could not overload me, because the Father in me doeth the work.

I allow myself to rest in the quietness of God in me, for He in me is greater than anything in the outer world. Every cell of my body nods assent to this prayer, and responds to the new flow of spiritual energy coming direct from the Father.

While writing these pages, I received a joyous telephone call from a man whose prolapsed colon has returned to normal and whose hemorrhoids have subsided after years of futile doctoring. Hemorrhoids are only veins that have succumbed to the picture of overload; a prolapsed colon suffers the same burden. The man reports that he has dissolved his belief in overload and is allowing God to think His adequacy through him.

The Problem of the Alcoholic

Mr. and Mrs. Alkow came in to see me one day when I was giving some lectures in San Francisco. They were alcoholics. They were a sensitive, intelligent couple, deeply ashamed of their habit. He had had several brushes with the police and his driver's license had been taken away. She had developed a serious liver ailment.

They had taken "cures," had placed signs around various rooms in their home with the declaration, "I won't touch the cursed stuff," and other lines equally emphatic. They had attended excellent Alcoholics Anonymous sessions, had been prayed with by their pastor and had been converted in revival meetings. They had tried every means they could think of, but the old habit returned each time.

The Yale Studies on Alcoholism had brought out the fact that a frontal attack on this problem rarely is successful. This I pointed out to them. Gritting the teeth, setting the will, and fighting the habit directly are invitations to defeat.

It is becoming clear that excessive drinking is not the chief problem. The drinking is only a symptom; the underlying cause is emotional and spiritual. When this is healed, the impulse and the desire for excessive drinking fall away. In most cases there is no direct struggle.

The chief cause of alcoholism is a sense of inadequacy, frustration, defeat, or insufficiency, usually accompanied by a rebellious disposition. It is difficult to uncover this because it is usually completely unrecognized. Each person has his own explanation of the reasons for his drinking and as usual the self-diagnosis is wrong; therefore, the treatment is wrong.

We All Want to Win

Psychologists tell us that every one of us is possessed of an *unconscious* will to live and a will to die; a will to win and a will to lose; a will to acquire and a will to throw away. These unconscious drives determine our attitudes toward life.

Man was made for living, winning, acquiring. The law of life is "Adapt, change, and win." Even the grocery store that does not adapt to meet changing conditions will eventually fail.

We come of a winning biological strain. We are the top-quality descendants of the finest ancestors. As the stream of life developed, only those survived who could adapt and change; those who failed to do this through stupidity or cowardice were snuffed out before maturity.

Therefore, only the successful grew to maturity and begat progeny. Thus the people on earth today are the products of a naturally selected strain of winners. In our blood is the accumulated will to win of thousands of generations of winning ancestors. We are intended for winning, not for losing. We are equipped for winning.

This is why we hate to lose, to feel inferior. This is why we prefer prosperity to stringency, health to illness, recognition to obscurity. To be snubbed or humiliated in front of others hurts deeply because it suggests that we are less than others. The stream of life in us urges us forward to victory and failure of any sort is an indication that we are out of the center of the stream, stagnated in an eddy.

The "name-dropper" is one who seeks to bolster his inward insecurity by tying himself with one who is more prominent. The small fry who crowd about the champion and shine in his reflected glory lose no time in transferring their insincere adulation to the new champ. Not being winners in their own right, they must constantly fasten themselves like pilot fish to some bigger fish. It is an unconscious urge, an impulse from the overcoming ancestors in their blood.

We do not censure them for this, because we recognize that their actions spring from an unconscious urge to be associated with the winner.

Many persons shrink from engaging in competition because of the fear of failure. They hold back from athletic competition, or continue working for another, fearing to open up in business for themselves. They settle down into minor jobs instead of going for the more important positions. The fear of failure in the timid outweighs the desire for wealth or fame. They dread the idea of losing; therefore, they don't dare start. Our fear of failure is only the obverse side of our will to win.

The Alcoholic's Imaginary Victory

The will to win, coupled with the will to die, is at the root of alcoholism. Somewhere in the alcoholic's deeper thought area is either a realization of failure or a fear of it. Alcohol has two effects in the brain. It stimulates it, then puts it to sleep. In the stimulated phase the person moves up to the level of the winner. He often boasts, feels unrepressed, is emotionally and socially at ease, where before he may have been shy or reserved. He will attempt things from which he formerly shrank. He has great confidence in himself.

The words he speaks seem to him to be words of wisdom. He feels prosperous, leaves his change lying on the bar, gives big tips. He is as good as any man, or better. He may become quite pugnacious, tell the police officer to go chase himself. These are all exaggerated notions of greatness. He is an imaginary winner in his present state.

In certain drinkers, or at certain stages in all drinkers, the person may become withdrawn, surly, and uncommunicative. Eventually, he "passes out." Now he is "dead to the world." All his troubles are over. He is no longer nagged by the thought of his inadequacy. During his exalted stage, he has satisfied the will to win without actually winning; now he has satisfied the will to die, without actually dying, for he has passed into unremembering oblivion.

The entire procedure is emotional from start to finish. Thus psychosomatic medicine is correct in declaring that alcoholism is a mental rather than a physical disease. It has been demonstrated that the physical tissues do not of themselves develop a physical craving for alcohol. The craving is a perversion of the craving for mastery. Thus a frontal attack on the actual drinking of liquor leaves the underlying *parent thought* of inadequacy untouched. Will power fails because it is directed against the wrong target.

How the Illusion of Separation Begins

This was a revelation to the unhappy Alkows and it led to their complete emancipation. We had several interviews, trying to trace back to the source their feelings of inadequacy. The woman found the root of her problem quickly. All her life she had felt inferior to her sister, a brilliant, beautiful girl two years older. Mrs. Alkow was the ugly duckling of the family, only a fair student and quite stout. Her sister was besieged for dates while she received no invitations. Finally married to the only man who ever took her out, she lived in constant dread lest he would see her as she saw herself and would leave her. She had forced herself to drink with him in order to hold him.

His tracing also led to something interesting. He recalled that one day when he was about five years old, his family had company. Somehow he had amused the visitors by his antics. He was cavorting around the living room, becoming more of a show-off as they laughed, when his father entered without the boy seeing him. The first thing he knew, he was receiving a hard slap on the mouth from his father and he still remembers his father's words, "You d——— little show-off. You think you're smart, but you're dumb as h———. Get out and wash your dirty neck."

The unexpectedness of the blow and the bitter acid of the words burned deep into his memory. He said that even in later years he would wake up in the night trembling at their recollection. He had always wondered why he shrank from competition. When angry he could fight and whipped boys older and heavier; but when the athletic director at the university saw him in a fight, and pleaded with him to enter the boxing tournament for the honor of the school almost guaranteeing that he would win, he shrank from the idea.

He entered the sales field in Chicago and compiled an outstanding record. Within three years, he was offered the managership of his firm's Detroit office, a position of prestige and larger income. But he felt afraid of the responsibility. He turned it down, yet was surprised to find himself hating the man who took the job. At about this time, his social drinking progressed to the point where it became a problem. Incidentally, he was drunk when he proposed to his wife, and didn't have the heart to hurt her by withdrawing when he realized what he had done. However, her fine inward qualities had drawn his love through the years. They seemed ideally suited to one another.

Space forbids detailing the downward path of this couple. He lost his good job and they roamed the country from coast to coast, sometimes doing well, most often on the ragged edge.

What Alcohol Does, Right Thinking Can Do Better

During our interviews we talked of the fact that under the influence of liquor he felt that he could whip the world. I showed him that this proved his mind's capacity to rise to that level. It could be brought up to that level again without the influence of alcohol. The next step would be to find out which particular series of ideas would most quickly bring back his inward sense of adequacy and sufficiency.

He was an intelligent man and cooperated well as we worked out his scheme. First, he measured himself against other men physically. Six feet tall, well built, good-looking, he was above the average of the men he met.

He knew that he could talk well. He could sell and he was honest in his presentation of a product. He felt superior to many salesmen in these particulars.

He recalled his previous successes. In recent years these had made him bitter. He had felt as if he were forever separated from his accomplishments. But he now began to cultivate a warm feeling toward them, as if he were still in their center. To remove his resentment he talked to himself about the man who had taken the manager's job in Detroit, telling himself what a fine fellow he had been and wishing him the greatest success.

He forgave his father, freely and unreservedly, even though the father had passed on. He blessed his memory. He did the same for various persons at whom he had become embittered during the years. It was a thorough mental catharis. The man was being born again.

The Infinite Takes Care of Its Own

Mr. and Mrs. Alkow exerted every effort to absorb themselves in the beautiful. They said that this regimen held them steady on a few occasions when they were tempted to take "just one."

Living as they did, they found that the natural outcome of their lives was joy. In previous years they had not laughed much, so they carefully cultivated the spirit of happiness. If they had to refuse door-to-door peddlers, they did so cheerfully, not sharply. They learned to see the comical side of things they once would have called tragedies.

Some of these procedures may seem to be inconsequential, but a large consciousness is made up of many small features, and "the little foxes spoil the vines." Many persons refrain from the big sins but spoil life by a multiplicity of small sins.

The motive from which Mr. and Mrs. Alkow followed these procedures is more important than what they did. They resolved not to block the outflow of any of God's qualities through themselves so far as was humanly possible. They believed that they did not have to struggle and strain to reproduce the qualities of God in their lives;

the Infinite was trying to do this constantly anyway. All they did was to let God express His nature through them.

They have become solid supporters of the church they joined, but without becoming religious nuisances to anyone. Their neighbors welcome them as a well-balanced couple. He has become a successful salesman. They have had eleven years of real living since the change.

HAVE YOU EVER SAID:

"I can't go through with it!"

HAVE YOU EVER SAID:

"This is more than I can bear!"

That type of expression indicates that the parent thought of *overload* is dominating you.

THINK:

I am adequate to anything that can happen.

Nothing is too much for me, because nothing is too much for God, whose thoughts now dwell in my mind.

chapter nine

Nothing Is Ever Lost

MISS PERDIDO WAS ABOUT FIFTY WITH THAT MOST ATTRACtive combination—a young face, sensitive patrician features, and beautiful gray hair.

She opened the interview by saying: "I have heard you say that no one can take anything away from us without our consent. Well, I have just received word that I have been cheated out of my estate.

"My father repeatedly told my two sisters and me that he wanted his property to go to me. He showed us his will, and in it he had left 10 per cent to each of my sisters, who are married to rich men, and 80 per cent to me because I am single. It was not a large estate. My share would have been just enough to enable me to live quietly for the remainder of my life.

"But the will has mysteriously disappeared, and now

the court has decided that the estate is to be divided equally among us. My third will not enable me to live. I shall have to continue my work as a teacher in a private school. It is all I know and it is poorly paid work. It is not only that I am in financial need. I think that I could adjust to that; but the inconsiderate selfishness of my sisters overwhelms me. I have pleaded with them to carry our my father's wishes, since they do not need the money, but they have refused."

I explained that it still is true that no one can take anything from us without our consent, but that she had unwittingly given her consent by her basic attitudes. Her misfortune could not have occurred to her unless she had somewhere developed a fundamental belief in *loss*.

The Parent Thought *that Brings* Loss

The *parent thought* of *loss* is widespread, yet so subtle that few persons realize they harbor it. It causes some of the unhappiest experiences, in which people lose property, friends, jobs, love. It also shows up in a number of physical conditions.

As we talked, it gradually dawned upon Miss Perdido that she had accepted this belief in loss from her youngest days. It would probably have taken long work by a skilled psychoanalyst to uncover its source in her. The following incident might not have led to its inception, but it undoubtedly was part of the general picture.

She recalled that when she was about seven her parents had brought her a beautiful doll on their return from a business trip to Spain. It was an expensive doll with almost lifelike features, and beautifully dressed.

Since her sisters were some years older and she had no

other playmates, she had poured her love into the doll. She would "take it on trips" around the garden, sing to it, fuss with it, tell it stories. She could not go to sleep at night without it.

As the family was returning home from church one rainy Sunday, the horses ran away, the carriage was wrecked, the family suffered minor injuries, and in the ensuing confusion no one remembered the doll. The next day a careful search failed to recover it. It had probably been picked up and carried away.

The child was inconsolable. The doll had been so much a part of her that the sense of loss was almost unbearable. As she had never been emotionally sturdy, this experience cut deep and left its mark. The *parent thought* of loss was on its way.

She recalled that all her life she had lost things. When she had completed a thesis on her major subject in college, she had left it on a restaurant table. When she returned looking for it two hours later, no one had seen it. She had no copy and was forced to do the work all over again in order to graduate. Her fiancé went overseas in World War I, but met and married a French girl. She detailed loss after loss, culminating in the loss of her father's estate.

What Thought Has Caused, Thought Can Cure

"But," she asked me, "does this mean that I am to pass the remainder of my life losing everything upon which my heart is set?"

"Not at all! That which our thought has done our thought can undo. A false belief can always be replaced by a true one, once we know what we wish to cultivate.

"In the truest sense, there is no loss in the universe. We call a thing lost when it has gone out of our possession without our conscious desire. But it has not gone out of existence. It is somewhere. Let us say that I have 'lost' my pen. That means that I cannot lay my hands on it. But it is lying in a gutter, or under some papers, or perhaps reposing in someone else's pocket by this time.

"Since we arrive at any desired condition in life by seeing it as a condition of Infinite Mind, we should remember that the pen is not lost to the Mind of God. Nothing is ever lost to that Mind, which surrounds and indwells every particle of matter anywhere throughout the universe; therefore it can safely be assumed that God has neither belief in nor fear of loss.

"We have said that one can experience only that in which he believes. Then if one can heal this fundamental belief in loss, he will stop suffering loss. There are many persons who never lose anything. They simply have rid themselves of all belief in loss as a part of their experience.

"When we fear loss, we fear that we are not capable of reproducing within ourselves that which God is in Himself. This is a denial of our basic nature. For however imperfect the image may be, the fact remains that man is made in the image and likeness of God. Perhaps none of us will be able perfectly to reproduce the nature of God, but this does not excuse us from trying. If we can raise our level of belief and acceptance even a notch or two, this corrected belief will show itself in definite results."

Do Not Consent to Loss

"Now, suppose we start on the matter in this way:

You want the security that would have come from this estate. Very well. Let us try to induce the belief that no one can rob any of us of our good without our consent. In the past you have actually given your consent, by believing in and accepting loss. So you can start right now by definitely *withdrawing* your consent from any future experience of loss.

"You might not feel any strong conviction in this direction at first. But conviction tends to grow after we have made a definite *choice*. *Any* type of thought, definitely *chosen* and steadily adhered to, will ultimately be accepted and worked upon in our deeper mental levels. This is a law of mind. It will work as well *for* you as in the past it has worked against you.

"A belief in *fulfillment* automatically dissolves out a belief in loss. At your present stage, security would be fulfillment. I am not going to ask you to forget money; that would be too much. But let it recede into the background, and bring the idea of *fulfillment* into the foreground as often as you are able.

"See yourself now as a part of the Mind of God. Tell yourself how incongruous it would be for God's Mind to be thinking in two contradictory directions. Think as God thinks, singlemindedly. Make yourself part of God's fulfillment by thinking in this way:

I and the Father are one; therefore I surrender my imperfect thinking. I am going to let this Mind that was in Christ Jesus be in me, thinking Its thoughts through me. These thoughts are thoughts of fulfilled desire since all of God's desires are always being fulfilled. The Lord is my Shepherd; I shall not want for any good thing. He restoreth my soul, my thinking; I will fear no evil and I will *choose* to dwell in this house of the Lord forever.

"Whether your security comes through the finding of the will or through some hitherto unthought-of channel is not important. But according to your faith it will come."

The will has never been found. But two weeks after our interview, Miss Perdido was asked to escort an English educator through the private school. Four months later they were married. He said that after losing his wife in an air raid years before he had never seen anyone who had interested him, but that he had been impressed by Miss Perdido's tranquil self-possession, which rested him and brought him the first inner peace in years. Her newfound belief in fulfillment had borne its results.

Life is never unfair. Its seeming harshness is only the consequence of our belief. Life's law is always "learn or suffer."

One Loss Accepted Brings Others

Sometimes *parent thoughts* develop as the result of one scorching experience. The following is an instance of the impact of a single staggering blow.

Mr. and Mrs. Bliss had been married for twenty-seven years. He owned his own business. They were pals, went everywhere together. She had worked alongside him when the business was getting started. Now, when they were in their fifties, their eyes would meet with the same fondness that they had known in their early years. Their three children, reared in that delightful atmosphere, had made happy marriages.

Then the blow fell. He was struck down by a drunken driver and instantly killed. She was prostrated; she could not see anyone for some weeks; her children could not comfort her. She was not to be blamed for this, because in a united couple such grief was to be expected and time gradually brings us out from under such clouds.

But her grief became a morbid state. Within the following two or three years she would buttonhole her friends, saying, "Isn't it terrible that Ed was taken? I'll never get over his loss. Why should he have been taken when we were so happy? Others who quarrel and abuse their wives are left, but I had to lose him." Her continual harping on her loss gradually alienated many of her friends. Some accused her of playing for sympathy.

The business was sold and she had a nice income. But she got into the hands of a dishonest customer's man in a brokerage house, who unloaded on her all the "cats and dogs" he had in his own folio, and soon she was in a precarious financial condition.

One day she took off two very valuable diamond rings to wash her hands in a department store. When she rushed back, she found the room empty and no trace of the diamonds. She came to me with the old familiar question, "Why should I have lost my rings when I never feared losing them, never expected it? How could this have happened to me?"

I brought out the idea that one does not have to think of a particular condition in order to experience it. One entertains the *parent thought*; it produces its own offspring.

Blessings Counted Multiply

Mrs. Bliss made a beautiful recovery. "Counting her blessings," she pushed Ed's loss into the background. She drew into the foreground her three children and the grandchildren, her beautiful home, her friends, her health. She came into a new realization of life and its promise.

Better still, she came into a beautiful sense of oneness with the Father. Later she said, "All my life I had thought I was a Christian. Ed and I supported the church. I took part in its activities. For a few years I taught a girls' Bible class. But as I look back, I realize that there was never any sense of a real unity with God. I went through all the motions, but it was only theory—although I would have been deeply offended if anyone had dared suggest it.

"But now I have a sense of inseparable oneness with God. He is as real to me as Ed was, if I may say it with reverence. Now I live by the verse that says, 'That I may know Him and the power of His resurrection.' Formerly I only knew *about* Him; now I seem actually to know *Him*. I let Him do His thinking through me."

A department store porter attended a revival meeting shortly afterward and was converted. He confessed picking up her rings and disposing of them. An arrangement was made with the person who had bought them, so that she got them back. Not all, but some of the stocks that the broker had unloaded on her came back almost to the price level at which she had bought them, upon which she got rid of them because she did not want to have that period of her thought brought back to her.

I have noticed that lost things often are restored when one corrects the underlying *parent thought*. Sometimes they are not. But of one thing I am certain: One can bring into his life that which more than compensates for what has gone out. In numerous instances where one has lost love, where the ex-partner has married again and reunion is impossible, a beautiful new love has developed when the belief in loss has been blotted out. In cases where a job has been filled, the person has found his or her way into one as good or better.

Every Ending Is a Beginning

The important thing is that we look upon every ending as a beginning. Many persons concentrate upon what has gone out of their lives. This binds them in slavery to a repetition of loss. They would do better to cultivate the expectancy of that which is ready and willing to come into their lives.

Endings are endings only if we believe them to be. Doors that close can be doors closed forever. But for every door that closes, there is always another ready to open if one believes that it *can* open.

Every ending can be made into a new beginning. We can pick ourselves up from amid the wreckage of shattered hopes and build a brave new world, but we must build a brave new attitude first.

With what? Not with anything imaginary. There must be a dynamic-in-being to turn thoughts into things. There is only one Power in the wide universe that can do this. That Power is God.

THINK ON WHAT YOU HAVE,

NOT ON WHAT YOU HAVE LOST,

FOR

BLESSINGS COUNTED MULTIPLY

AND

EVERY LOST THING

CAN BE RESTORED

OR COMPENSATED FOR.

chapter ten

Let Yourself Be Loved

No tragedy is quite so poignant as that of the woman who is denied the fulfillment of her life through love and the making of a home. Love may be to some men a thing apart, but the poet spoke truth when he declared "it is woman's whole existence." To be passed by when men are seeking wives is not only a blow to a woman's pride; it is a cruel starvation of her deepest instincts. During my years of interviewing thousands of men and women, I believe that the most tragic have been those attractive, sincere, warmhearted women who have failed to draw lasting love into their lives. They would gladly pour all of their rich femininity into the life of some man; yet they seem doomed to an unattached life of loneliness.

Miss Reejeck was a schoolteacher, graduate of an excellent university. At twenty-seven she was an attractive brunette, with the face and figure of a model. She went for outdoor sports, enjoyed good music, loved to cook, and had strong maternal instincts. Very sincere, well-poised, gracious, she could have inspired any man on his way to the top.

"What is the matter with me?" she asked. "I know that I am not actually repulsive. I dance well, I'm not a gold-digger; yet my dates never get to the point of real seriousness. I get many propositions but no proposals. I have done more wrestling in cars than is done on television, but men drop me when they find out that I don't play that way. My two younger sisters are both happily married, although even they will admit that I present a better appearance.

"I've almost decided that if marriage is not for me I might as well play around on my dates as so many of my friends do. But this is not what I want. My parents have had a beautiful home life. Why can't I have the same fine, clean, decent experience?"

We Reject Ourselves, Then Blame Others

Miss Reejeck is typical of many. Some are older, less attractive, but most of them are women of excellent quality who would be a source of comfort and joy to most men.

They are usually surprised when I say: "The men are not passing you by. It is you yourself who are keeping them from seriously considering you. No one but you can change this situation, and changing it is quite within your power."

Rejection is one of the *parent thoughts* buried deepest in the race mind. It becomes active in people's lives in different ways. Very often it starts with some misunderstanding in childhood.

Correction and chiding are often necessary in the training of a child. The sensitive child sometimes misunderstands this. The expressions of disapproval on the parents' faces, the words of rebuke, the spanking, set up a fear in the child's mind that the parents have withdrawn from her, that they have pushed her out of their love. The more sensitive the child, the deeper the groove cut in her thinking. Unconsciously she comes to see rejection in the childish hostile attitudes of her playmates, in the stern censure of her teachers. Gradually it develops into a strong-running stream in the deeper levels of her thought life. It has become an actively operating *parent thought*.

Years pass; the original experience is forgotten; yet "the melody lingers on." Constantly rising from the cellar of her mind is the feeling that she is not wanted, that people do not approve of her, that she is not attractive, that her gifts and good qualities are very ordinary. Sometimes she struggles to excel. She may become proficient in scholarship, athletics, or the arts. But such external excellences are not so deeply rooted as her unconscious feelings of rejection. The young woman is puzzled at her failure to achieve an inner sense of oneness with others.

The Mysterious Feeling of Unworthiness

The belief in rejection is coupled with an inexplicable feeling of unworthiness. Unless it is healed, she marries beneath her level; or if on her own level, she is plagued by the constant fear of losing her husband's love. This fear can lead into an unreasonable jealousy which of itself is sufficient to make her fears come true. In the business world it leads to loss of the job.

This fear of rejection can be born out of ridiculously insignificant items. Miss Reejeck thought that it might be traced back to a bathing suit. When she was four years old her little cousin went with the family to the beach. The parents took along an extra bathing suit; it was an old one that was faded and torn. When they got to the beach, they gave the nice suit to her cousin and forced their daughter to use the ugly suit. She said that she cried herself to sleep that night because she thought her parents didn't love her any more. To our mature minds this was ridiculous; we must remember that to the young child it was quite logical.

We cannot always trace the origin of our false concepts. But we may be assured that sometime, somewhere, there is always a beginning to disordered thought patterns.

The psychologist might encourage the person to live through the original experience, meanwhile laughing at it from the exalted point of view of adulthood. This is sometimes helpful. But I usually suggest a different procedure.

Knowing that the basic *parent thoughts* are the cause of all negative experience, I explained to Miss Reejeck that her life had been lived under the compulsion of a lie. Neither her parents, her playmates, nor her teachers had had any desire to reject her. She had misinterpreted their attitudes and her life had been lived in a totally false belief. This lie upon which she had acted had kept her from life's fulfillment.

But the false belief had been kept alive only by her faith in it. She could destroy it by building a new belief in her acceptability.

"But I've tried all this," she objected. "I've told myself that I am attractive. I've measured myself against other girls. I've tried to convince myself that there is no reason why I should not draw the love they have drawn. But it has not done any good."

"Suppose we shift the emphasis a little," I replied. "I believe that only two changes are necessary. First, we shall start from a different basis, and second, we shall introduce a new and different power-factor into the situation.

Love Thinks First of the Other Person

"Marriage is a two-way contract. We get and we give. Perhaps your thought has been too much on what you would get. Many salesmen never succeed until they move beyond this point. It is right that their minds should be on the commission they will receive, but a man becomes a real salesman only when he bases his proposition on a decided benefit to his prospect.

"We can pass by the enumeration of your good points. You are already aware of them. But suppose we think of the ways in which your particular sort of girl can meet the needs of some particular sort of man.

"Marriage is not only the coming together of a man and a woman. It is a blending of two personalities so dovetailed into each other that they make a perfect unit. That which he lacks, you have. That which you lack, he has.

"Hours, months and years are to be spent together in which the sex element will be far in the background. In a perfect marriage, two personalities are held together by the unconscious amalgam of an unseen and unconscious communion of the soul. But so long as one of the partners clings to a deep-seated acceptance of rejection, this communion cannot be. And the insecure partner would be destroying the marriage while striving to maintain it.

"Let us say that you have made a profile of yourself. You have taken yourself just as you are. You have not exaggerated your charm nor toned down your less desirable points. You have looked yourself squarely in the face and decided that you are neither saint nor sinner. You are just you, a combination of the good and the bad.

"Now somewhere there is a man who has always held an ideal of the sort of girl he would like to marry, just as you have an ideal of the man you would like. This man has met many girls. He has been interested in some of them, but never enough to marry. His ideal picture has not yet appeared.

"You are that girl. You are no better nor any worse than others he has met. But you fit the partly unconscious picture he has always held. You might reproduce in his mind his own mother or some schoolteacher he adored when he was six years old, for often men marry an early image of desirability.

"In a very real sense, you are the only person who can ever completely fulfill life for him. If he becomes discouraged waiting for that certain girl to come along, he might decide to marry anyway; but that girl will never completely fill the bill for him. He might remain faithful to her for fifty years, but she will never have met his deepest need. Only you can do that, not because you are more gifted or attractive, but because what you are inside dovetails exactly with what he is inside, in some subtle, elusive manner or by some intangible quality of mind and soul.

"This man needs you, wants you, wishes he could find you. You need no tricks to 'catch' him, no schemes to hold him. In one sense we might say that your marriage has already been made in heaven, even though it is the fashion to sneer at the phrase.

"Think of the peace of mind, the deepest satisfactions, the feeling of fulfillment you alone can bring to him, apart altogether from the physical side of marriage. Think of the new interest in his work, the plans and ideals for the family that grip a man who otherwise might drift along in a humdrum career. This is what you give while you are getting the rewards of his companionship."

The Best Comes to Those Who Believe in It

"Yes," she replied, "but aren't you picturing the ideal situation? This is the kind of marriage one reads about in a novel. How often do you find it in real life? I have reached the stage where I believe that I would be satisfied with half a loaf."

"You don't have to be satisfied with anything less than the best. But there is one condition: you have to believe that you can *have* the best. You have to cultivate the belief that in this two-way contract called marriage you and you alone are the person who can bring fulfillment to this man.

"Deliberately close your ears to everything you may hear about 'getting your man,' about the women outnumbering the desirable men, about the difficulty of holding a man once you have him. Ignore the hundred and one clichés that women utter. These may all be true for those who speak them, because that is what they believe. You, however, refuse to believe in them; therefore, they have no power to operate in your love life."

The Invisible Matrimonial Agent

"Now for the new power factor in the situation. Your ideal for marriage did not originate in you. The Infinite Mind streaming through you carries all levels of pictures. Your particular degree of sensitiveness has failed to catch the grosser levels; you have caught the finer levels. This is one reason why you have not brought yourself to the point of playing around with love. That same level, registered by some man, has made him reluctant to tie his life to those he has so far met.

"God is the perfect Knower. He knows where you are and where a man of like caliber is. He knows how to unite gross with gross, and fine with fine, for His Law side is forever bringing together that which is in harmony and separating that which is not harmonious. There is not the slightest reason why He would put this ideal within you and then mock you. It is there because the Knower wants to see it fulfilled."

We prayed together and I suggested that she use a daily prayer treatment. It ran something like this:

I know that I have believed a lie in thinking that I was ever rejected by anyone. I know that I am greatly desired by the type of man who would fill my ideals. I know that he will never find true and lasting happiness until he finds it in me. He needs me just as truly as I need him. Neither one confers a one-sided benefit upon the other. Each gives and each gets.

The Infinite Knower knows where each of us is to-day. He is even now moving us across the chessboard of life so that we shall meet, and we shall recognize one another. I let go of all my tenseness, relinquishing the entire responsibility for the meeting to the Infinite Knower. I know that we shall know each other when we meet; that I am not in competition with anyone else for this man, and he is not in competition with anyone else for me.

He needs me, wants me, loves me, and all these emotions are returned by me. I release this whole situation to the Infinite Knower, giving thanks for its completion now, even before I see its manifestation.

Several months went by. She had several dates, none of which was satisfactory. She wavered a bit, but clung to her new-found attitude toward her problem. She said that she had released it all to the Infinite Mind, and that this had brought her a deep sense of inward serenity.

One day she was dining near the school with another teacher before going to some evening classes. A tall blond man seated nearby asked for directions to a certain theatre; he wanted to see a particular picture. The directions were somewhat complicated; this led to considerable discussion. He presented his card, said he had recently arrived from Sweden to go into business here, and asked if they would think him forward if he invited them to accompany him to see the picture. They were not too interested in the lecture they had intended hearing, so the trio set off for the theatre.

It has turned out beautifully. Her tall brunetteness matches his tall blondness; their tastes and ideals are similar. He has taught her to ski. Their auburn-haired daughter is almost two years old, and they have a home in which harmony reigns. I asked her if she had any feeling that he had done her a favor by taking her off the market. She laughed and said that he had picked up one Americanism of which he seemed to be particularly fond. It was "Baby, where have you been all my life?"

The Invisible Realtor

Mr. and Mrs. Moody had an apartment house for sale. They had worked hard, saved their money, and invested in this building thinking it would support them in their old age. But they found so many aspects of the renting business disagreeable that they wanted to get out. They put the apartment house up for sale. Many looked but no one bought.

They tried several brokers. Each one said he could not explain why their prospects remained cold after seeing the property. The price was not out of line. The income was satisfactory. It was a good investment.

After talking with the Moodys, I felt that both husband and wife held a deep-seated belief in the *parent thought* of rejection. As one of the ways to master this *parent thought*, I suggested that they try the following: Sit quietly, visualize the apartment house as it looks from the other side of the street. Admire it, love it, think how beautiful it looks. See men and women walking past it, then out of the crowd see one person stop, look it over carefully, walk up and down scanning it from every angle, then enter the front door to ask if it is for sale.

They were very conscientious people, and at first they demurred at my suggestion. They said it seemed like trying to hypnotize someone into buying.

I pointed out that the procedure was not for the purpose of influencing anyone but themselves. It was to be a little drill for them, leading them to the thought of acceptance, which would replace their belief in rejection. I also outlined a prayer treatment for them to use.

They had been trying unsuccessfully to sell the business for five months. Four or five days after our talk, they were in the lobby rearranging paintings on the walls when a man walked in. He said he had been looking for an apartment house in the vicinity and had been impressed by this particular building. He asked if it was for sale.

Within another week the sale was closed at a figure eminently satisfactory to both parties, and without a real-estate agent.

Here in substance was the prayer treatment:

This building is part of the Infinite Substance, and so are we. There is a buyer who wants exactly this type, size, and quality of building, in this neighborhood. He likes its appearance and feels that our price is fair. He sees it, investigates it, and he closes the deal.

There is nothing in either of us that denies the truth of what we are saying. Any long-lying sense of rejection is now being healed within us, as we invite the Infinite Healing Presence to dissolve it out. We live day by day in a real sense of acceptance. We are accepted by all whom we meet; our apartment house is likewise accepted at its value.

We turn ourselves and our business over completely to the Divine Agent, who knows where the buyer is and where we are. We let go of all our inner tensions. We bless this house. We bless every tenant. We bless everyone who walks past it. We bless whoever is the buyer.

This is our word, spoken in the quietness of our new faith. We release it completely to the Infinite Creative

145

Law which alone can turn our thought about it into things. We are thankful for its cooperative response to our belief and our word.

This was all. A changed belief about themselves and about life, and changed circumstances followed, as the grass follows the new rain. This instance could be multiplied in scores of similar cases. "It *is* done unto us as we believe."

Your Outlook Determines Your Income

A man in pitiful circumstances came to Jesus. His son was epileptic. The father told how he sometimes fell into the fire, and what a sad situation the lad was in. He ended by saying, "Master if Thou can'st do anything, have compassion on us, and help us."

He stressed what *Jesus* could or could not do, but Jesus turned it completely around and said, "If *thou* can'st believe, all things are possible to him that believeth." Jesus refused to accept the problem on the basis of His powers; he placed the solution in the area of the man's faith, which is the only place where problems can be solved.

It is true in business as in physical healing. He who fails in business must not look outside of himself for the cause; it lies within. The sale of property or goods, the winning of love, the advancement to higher responsibility in the business world, all come from the level of the person's consciousness, by the same principle that heals the body.

Change your outlook, and you can change your world.

*IF YOUR LIFE IS WITHOUT
LOVE THERE IS ONLY
ONE REASON.*

You have
rejected yourself

You are dominated by the parent
thought of rejection.

SOMEWHERE LOVE IS
WAITING FOR YOU.

Accept yourself as you are, accept
the world as it is and the Creative
Process will bring that love into
your life.

chapter eleven

Your Obedient Servant

PERHAPS THE BIGGEST HURDLE FOR THE NEWCOMER IS OUR statement of the absolute obedience of the Creative Law. It seems amazingly presumptuous to him that frail man could possibly direct God into action. The early religious training of most of us has conditioned us to believe that God is awesome, that He must be approached with fear and trembling, or at least with reverence, and that any attempt to tell God what to do must meet with a rebuff.

The Body Is Biased toward Health

The fact of the matter is that the Infinite is forever working toward a balanced perfection; God is always trying to express at the highest level. Illness is ugly imbalance; it is imperfection. All the acts of God reveal a bias toward health. What the doctor calls the recuperative self-healing power of the body is God's desire for a perfect body through which to express. Therefore, what we call "directing the Creative Law into action" is simply our aligning ourselves with what It already wants to do.

We are not bullying or bossing. We form a more perfect thought pattern to replace the ill-formed one that has brought about illness, then we present this to the Law side of the Infinite so that It can engage Itself with this more acceptable picture. It is reasonable then to assume that It delights to flow into the perfect mold.

This built-in bias toward health that the body manifests is an encouraging feature to those who practice spiritual healing. It has been observed that the body can stand a terrific amount of abuse. The effects of faulty diet, bad habits, overstrain, accidents, and gunshots, which should have carried the person to his grave, are thrown off, the body often making astounding recovery. Badly damaged hearts and ruined digestions amaze physicians by continuing to function when by all the laws of morbid pathology the patient should have died.

Just as the naval architect builds into a ship that tendency to fight back onto an even keel after it has been laid almost on its side by wind and sea, so the body fights its way back onto an even keel after storms that should have sunk it.

We know that the body has no intelligence of itself. Whence then came this indomitable tendency to fight back onto an even keel? It could have come from nowhere but from the Infinite Architect who designed it. And we can confidently assume that the Creative Law welcomes *any* effort to direct it in restoring normalcy.

God Does Not Condemn Us

We must correct the mistaken belief that man lies under God's condemnation or censure. The myth of the fall of man is a relic of a bygone theology. It is a generally accepted scientific fact that man is an evolving being, in whom reason slowly developed. He is on an upward, not a downward, path. If anything, the Father should be pleased that the son has come so far in so short a space of geological time. Millions of His children have already grasped their privileges and are living on a more or less stable level of oneness with the Father. That they fail sometimes is no dishonor, nor is it a sign of "original sin."

Man is never condemned for his failure to live up to the divine standard, any more than he is to be condemned when he spells *cat* k-a-t, or adds nine and eight and gets an answer of fourteen. These childish errors are not the result of an innate wickedness or perversity; they are the result of incomplete knowledge. Humans are children in the school of life, and through their mistakes they learn to do their arithmetic correctly.

Man is the latest living form to appear in the world. Scientists tell us that modern man arrived just one second ago in geological time. He has scarcely had time to look around and find out who he is, whence he came, and whither he is bound. This is seen by some of his ridiculously naïve concepts of God of less than three hundred years ago; they led him to think that he should torture men into the true faith and burn eccentric old women for witchcraft. They depicted a monstrous God who would burn people forever unless they subscribed to a particular ecclesiastical creed, no matter how blameless their lives.

The old false beliefs about God block man's progress toward freedom. But some people are deeply afraid to view truth from a new angle. Their spiritual mentors terrify them with warnings about the eternal consequences of "turning from the faith." Thus they are held in bondage to illness, poverty, unhappiness. They fail to realize "the glorious liberty of the children of God."

In this book I often use terms for God that are not Bible terms; yet they throw light on some phase of God's character that is necessary in understanding Him. I sometimes use familiar Bible verses with a different interpretation, one that my experience has shown bears directly upon life. I present a view of Jesus in which I depict His human and His divine sides as being representative of the human race.

The Secret of Abundant Life

Since the object of salvation is the reunion of God and man, Jesus did His best to show men how to become reunited with God through their thought, stressing the fact that all the gifts of life grow out of union with the Giver. His sense of union was so vivid, so alive, so intense, and so productive in its results that he could unequivocally say, "I and the Father are one."

Some theologians have denuded Christ's life of its potency for us by saying that He alone had authoritative power to set spiritual healing law in motion, for He was the Son of God. True, He was Son of God, but we have also been told, "Now are we sons of God." He promised us, "The works that I do shall ye do also, and even greater works shall ye do." He said further, "These signs shall follow them that believe . . . they shall cast out devils . . . they shall lay hands on the sick and they shall recover . . ."

If orthodoxy consists in following the commands and the example of the Christ, no church leader is orthodox who does not include authoritative healing of the sick through an understanding of the same spiritual law through which Jesus healed. It is heresy to deny that Jesus meant His disciples to be healers also.

The religious leader who says that healing was a special dispensation of the first century to enable the church to get started distorts the central theme of Jesus' teachings. He completely misrepresents the purpose of Jesus' life, for which He was willing to go to His death. He robs humanity of the one proved method of escaping bondage. He closes the door of heaven in the face of His followers. For heaven is not a place. It is a life of union with God, which leads to dominion over everything arising out of man's earth nature.

In union with God there is no sickness, want, unhappiness, or discord.

Jesus never took part in squabbles over orthodoxy. He was too broad-gauged in His view of life. His severest condemnation was visited upon the Pharisees who spent their time splitting theological hairs while their parishioners floundered helplessly in sin, illness, and misery. He said, "I am come that ye might have life and that ye might have it more abundantly." This was His sole aim, to teach men the secret of a happy life.

Belief Means Healing, Not Just Preaching

Throughout the ages, there have always been spiritual healings. Somewhat sporadic in character, they were usually attributed to some mysterious "gift" of healing possessed by certain individuals. Jesus tried to show that this was not so. He stated emphatically that the power to heal lay in one's belief.

Unfortunately, as in most human institutions, the original fire, fervor, and clear understanding of the principle were dissipated. The church became powerful and rich, outward form and ceremony were substituted for inner light, and these vital truths, which were of the heart to the heart, were largely lost. Emphasis then shifted to outward spoken or written creed. The Inquisition replaced Pentecost. Statements of theological theories took the place of a daily experience of the Universal living through the personal, and the descent into the Dark Ages was certain. To this day, sadly enough, those in various branches of the church who cannot grasp the principle not only omit but fight against the practice of spiritual healing.

The churches will never pass away. They have been of too much value to men. But their emphasis will change. Already they are moving away from theological discussions, replacing them with subjects that bear upon today's problems. In the near future, they will bear down more heavily on this scientifically spiritual approach to healing. Many are already doing it.

In Denver, Colorado, there is a courageous minister with good practical sense and lofty spiritual vision. Dr. Robert A. Russell is Rector of Epiphany Episcopal

Church. Through extensive study of the Bible, Dr. Russell was brought to the realization that Jesus did more healing than preaching. He searched deeply into psychological methods and found that some of them possessed a certain value, but that they lacked the distinctly spiritual note that Jesus struck.

Dr. Russell began to lay emphasis on this practical side of Jesus' teaching. Some outstanding healings took place. Then he decided to build The Shrine of the Healing Presence. Starting with a donation of a few dollars, he has constructed a beautiful edifice into which has gone more than three hundred thousand dollars, and in which this modern presentation of an ancient truth has resulted in the healing of body, soul, and mind for many hundreds of persons.

Dr. Russell has taught this truth to groups of Episcopal ministers. They are no less true to their church, but they have added the message of spiritual healing to their doctrinal teaching.

For several summers, Dr. Russell has brought his message to our theatre audience during my vacation. Sometimes the congregation is so large that we have to lease another theatre nearby for the overflow, for he is a dynamic speaker and his teaching of these methods is as clear as the note of a bell.

The church will be filled again when its ministers catch the vision and understanding of men like Dr. Robert A. Russell. It will not need to show movies to attract an audience.

The Infinite Wants to Express through Man

This chapter opened with the statement that the Creative Law wants to heal, is obedient to our word, and is quite willing to move in with all of its tremendous force whenever the heart is thrown open to its healing currents.

The chief thing to be assured of is that the Infinite seems eager to manifest Himself at the highest possible level. The outthrust of life that makes the tree root lift a concrete pavement or split a rock is the same Infinite desire that would break through the manmade barriers of illness, poverty, and unhappiness. There is no need to overcome the reluctance of an unwilling God. The Healing Principle intensely wishes to express Itself. All It needs is to receive that directive word and It rushes in to obey.

In the beginning, when It heard that word of God saying "let there be," It responded by bringing a world into form. Today, when It hears man say "let there be," It is hearing the same word of God, for man is only the channel through which God speaks. So in a sense, it is not *we* who order the Law into action. It is not *we* who thought up the idea of the Divine Perfection. We are the channel through which the Infinite speaks. But since we have the faculty for God-consciousness, we have become intelligent, self-conscious cooperators with God. This is the Supreme Partnership: "I and the Father are one," but "my Father is greater than I."

Sir James Ritchie, of the University of Edinburgh, speaking before the British Society for the Advancement of Science, drew a chart that should make for optimism regarding man's possibility of rapid mastery of spiritual law in the near future.

He drew a clock face on the board; he pointed out that life on this planet commenced at twelve midnight.

Each minute represented over one and a half million years as the clock of life steadily ticked its way around the dial. At ten-thirty A.M. fish were the highest form of life yet developed. At eleven-thirty, life had succeeded in producing only the reptiles. By eleven-forty-five, the mammals were beginning to appear. At eleven-fifty-nine our human ancestors were making their appearance or getting ready to appear, and at eleven-fifty-nine and fifty-nine seconds, modern man had arrived.

The thirty thousand years or so that modern man has been here may seem very long, and some are discouraged because he has made little inner progress during that time. But it is very brief compared with the long, slow, upward progress of the living forms that preceded us and that seemed necessary for our emergence.

We are on a journey of self-discovery. Throughout the geological ages the Infinite Intelligence has apparently sought constantly higher expression. Both philosophers and scientists are now coming into agreement that this is the only rational explanation of creation at all. Infinite Mind evidently intended the creation to be His organ of expression. It would be incorrect to believe that He has changed his plan from time to time, disappointedly discarding form after form until He hit upon the idea of man.

On the contrary, the end was known from the beginning. From the simple to the complex structure, all is part of the one plan. A baby could be born fully developed at the moment of conception, just as a new cell is created in a moment by fission. But apparently God works through an unfolding process which the scientist calls evolution. The child in nine unborn months begins as a single cell, becomes more complexly intricate during the months, passes through and recapitulates the biological history of the race from invertebrate to vertebrate, lives for a short time in all the species preceding the human, even showing gill slits like a fish at one stage. Since Infinite Intelligence was in that male and female cell fused into one, He continued to indwell all the succeeding forms on a constantly rising level until a human child was born. Why? Only God knows!

Infinite Intelligence never rushes things. Man is impatient; he wants perfection now. He wants all the sorrows of mankind to be dissolved out now. He wants men to be sweet, beautiful, and kind now. He sometimes wonders why God doesn't interfere to stop war and other horrors; he wonders whether God cares. If he only knew it, God would stop all these things right now, but He can only do *for* men what He does *through* them.

God's Progressive Emergence in Nature

God is able to express only at the level of the medium through which He is expressing. The rocks give God a certain mode of expression. Insensate, they could not give a sensory expression; yet the electrons of which they are composed whirl as correctly as those in the brain of a genius, because the Infinite Thinker thinks through that rock.

The vegetable kingdom is higher in the scale. Infinite Intelligence finds a higher level of expression in plants. They are not to be blamed for not thinking like men; yet there is a certain groping intelligence in the way they send their roots searching for minerals and moisture, and in the

156

way they turn their leaves toward the sun. Of course, in neither rock nor plant is there self–conscious intelligence. It is all the One Thought of the One Thinker, thinking through them at their level of reception.

The animal kingdom gives a still higher medium of expression. Simple reasoning processes show here. The animal can run away from danger and make his way toward food. Whereas the Infinite had to take care of the sex life of plants, carrying the pollens on the winds, the animal can now find his own way toward procreation. But the animal does not know why he does certain things; they are the thoughts of the Infinite Thinker passing through his brain. This brain, being simple in its structure, can allow God's All-Knowledge a somewhat limited expression.

Man prides himself upon being the highest of the four kingdoms. And he is! His brain is a thing of amazing complexities. That rind of the brain, the cortex, about one-eighth of an inch thick, is said to have more than two billion separate thinking cells, each of which can combine with any other of the two billion to form a separate and distinct kind of thought. By these combinations man is capable of quintillions of separate ideas. He is a superb organ for the Infinite expression.

Man Is the Ideal Channel for God

The thoughts of God can mingle with the thoughts of man better than with anything else in the universe. This is what makes man's mind the ideal channel for the Healing Process.

The rocks of the mineral kingdom might be said to have no consciousness of their own. The vegetable kingdom has little more, yet there must be some dim sort of consciousness of sunlight, soil, and water. The animal has a more extended consciousness and a decided self-consciousness; it is aware that it is something separate from other animals.

Man has both self- and God-consciousness. "God sleeps in the rock, becomes conscious in the plant, self-conscious in the animal, and God-conscious in man." This statement has been variously attributed to the German, the Greek, and the Hindu, but it is clearly the statement of discriminating thinkers.

In man, the Creator has at last come to the place for the fullest outpouring of all of His ideas. It must be remembered that just as it was the Original Thinker thinking through the electrons in the rock, the plant, the animal, so what man calls his own thought is still the thought of the Infinite Thinker. True, man's brain is involved in the process. But the brain is only the violin upon which the Divine attempts to bring forth celestial harmonies. Throughout all creation, from simple to complex, all thought is God's thought.

Having evolved this complex thinking structure in man, the Infinite stands aside to allow man to discover himself and his potentialities. God will not pull aside the curtains of mystery. This is man's task. He is perfectly capable of knowing anything he wishes to know, but it must be along a pathway of self-discovery.

Throughout the ages, voices have always sounded the message of man's inner universe, the origin of power over his experiential life. Here is a field for exploration more thrilling than any part of the physical universe. These voices have spoken of values beyond those of immediate advantage, beyond the glitter of the material. But they have been drowned out by the rat-tat-tat of riveting machines building some new colossus of steel or by the strident voices and the mailed boots of the conquerors marching home from victory.

Now even the conqueror is afraid, or at least uncertain. He is beginning to wonder if there is not some better way. The human race stands at the crossroads of civilization, viewing its greatest menace and at the same time its most sublime opportunity. The world stands poised, ready today for its greatest forward step, that of an intensive exploration of its vast inner spiritual resources. I believe that it is about to take it.

The Mystery of Spiritual Hunger

The instinct for God is as true a part of man's nature as the instinct to eat or to mate. Instincts need not be taught; they are integral parts of us. The latter two, being physical, may be indulged in a gluttonous or animalistic manner. They become refined through the emergence of the first.

The hunger for food is necessary so that the individual organism will survive. The hunger for sex is necessary so that the species may survive. The hunger for God is necessary so that man shall be at home when he arrives at his true destination. The physical appetites are fleeting, the spiritual appetite is eternal. Spiritual appetite is of the inner invisible thinker, trapped for a few decades in physical form, but destined to break through into the ultimate freedom of a completely spiritual existence.

During those few decades of earth's kindergarten years, man needs the five physical senses. Living on a physical planet, he can make his way round only through the use of physical senses. But he also possesses spiritual feelers that constantly probe the spiritual world. He has a spiritual intuition that tells him, "If a man die he *shall* live again." Someone has said that man does not believe in immortality because he can prove it, but he tries to prove it because he cannot help believing in it.

What is this strange, otherworldly instinct that animates man alone in all the animal kingdom? The instinct for immortality is not a mockery; it is the voice of the Infinite in him. It continues to tell him that his life is much more than he can see, feel, and hear. It breathes gently in his ear, telling him that he is a far nobler being than his physical appetites would indicate. He comes from eternity. His destination is an eternity of continuing consciousness, for consciousness has its origin in the Eternal and can never die.

Man's ideals could not possibly have come from his lower ancestry. There is only one place from which they could have come—from their Absolutes hidden in the nature of the Infinite. Man did not originate them; he merely caught and registered them.

The purest love that man experiences, the highest delight in beauty, truth, or integrity that imperfect man experiences are only tiny scintillae of light from some harder-to-see Sun. Man catches a flashing gleam, loves it as an ideal, tries to live in its light. But it is only the relative virtue glancing from God the Absolute.

Man's spiritual ideals are the unwitting registration of

the Divine Ideal. Often dimly apprehended, this Voice of God in man is sufficient ground for believing that God is all that man's best is, and infinitely more. Man's concepts waver, sometimes the Light disappears for periods of time as the light from the lighthouse does to the sailors in a lifeboat making their arduous way toward it. But the Light Itself never wavers, for It is the Unchanging Reality toward which man journeys, and It is planted on solid ground.

Man's Voyage of Self-Discovery

But man must *choose* to know the truth. He has passed the stage of pre-humanity in which God did most of his thinking for him. He now has reason and intelligence sufficient to learn the facts about his relation to God and the mechanics of his own mind. He has been launched upon that river of exploration with the admonition, "Man, know thyself." He is on the pathway of self-discovery. His advance in health and happiness will now depend upon the wisdom of his deliberate choices.

Man's highest achievements in the mental and emotional realm will come only as he learns to use the "higher mathematics" of spiritual thinking. He already has all the mental equipment for it. Some daring souls are using this equipment with most gratifying results in their external affairs. And this newer approach is growing rapidly through one thing alone: the results that it is producing.

Something more potent than human argument is bringing this knowledge to the surface. The outward thrust of the Eternal is nudging man on to his manifest destiny. The purpose of life is that man shall know himself, his Divine origin, his almost incredible potentialities as a child of God and a co-worker with God.

The Infinite has manifested at the level of rock, plant, and animal. These were only the preliminary stages. The climax is now approaching, "the last for which the first was made." The Eternal will continue to express at the lower physical level through those who will not or cannot see a higher, for God never forces Himself on us. But in those who begin to tread this higher pathway to integration and its resultant well-being, the Healing Law will rush as air into a vacuum, for "Eye hath not seen, nor ear heard . . . the things which God hath prepared for them that love Him."

Reasons why the Creative Process will always work when you use it correctly.

▫ Infinite Intelligence is forever working toward a balanced perfection. Illness, trouble, and misery are ugly imperfections.

▫ Your own imperfect thoughts are blocking this tendency of your life to keep itself on an even keel.

▫ Get rid of these troublesome parent thoughts by replacing them with the clear vision of master thoughts.

▫ Then, the Creative Process will flow through you, bringing inevitable peace, accomplishment, and life-fulfilling happiness.

PART TWO

HOW TO USE THE CREATIVE PROCESS: *Methods, Techniques, and Sample treatments*

chapter twelve

How to Give a Healing

Prayer Treatment

ANYONE WHO CAN READ THIS BOOK CAN GIVE AN EFFECTIVE healing prayer treatment, either for himself or for another. There is nothing mysterious or highly technical about it.

First: Let him be convinced that when his treatment is given, it is not a shot in the dark; neither is it puny man storming the ramparts of heaven. It is the conscious setting in motion of a definite spiritual law, in a definite direction, to produce a specific effect. It is *a* thinker deliberately co-operating with *The* Thinker to place a thought pattern before the Creative Law—a thought pattern that the Law will *assuredly accept.* Moreover, that Law knows exactly what to do to change thoughts into things and will immediately move into appropriate action.

Second: The one who gives the treatment is not going to make a verbal assault on any disease, organ, or physical condition. Here is where many beginners go wrong. They treat an arthritic joint or a faulty heart, which are only the effects. The primary illness is in the thought life.

Knowing that the physical condition is thought taking form, the spiritual practitioner traces it back into thought and treats the thought. For if the *parent thought* is not eradicated, it can bring forth more and different offspring. "The demons finding the house empty swarm in again."

Third: One is best able to treat another by treating *himself*. In the truest sense we are not trying to influence or to change the thought of another. Treatment is for the purpose of convincing *ourselves* that the sick or defeated person has a false viewpoint on life, and that we are presenting the true state of affairs.

We Must Take God's View

Suppose we put it this way: We believe that the Infinite has a certain view of man and the whole creation. This view is one of perfection, right action and right functioning. The person who fails has somehow become possessed of a different, a contradictory view. This has resulted in his illness. God holds the true view; this one is holding a false view.

We, being human, have also a background of false beliefs about life. But our reason tells us that the sick person's view is wrong while that of the Infinite is right. Therefore, we determine to range ourselves on the side of divine Intelligence. So, we begin to convince ourselves that the true state of this person is that held by the Infinite.

To this end, we bring forth any arguments in support

of this position which will help us convince ourselves that we are "thinking God's thoughts after him."

When I give treatments, I often draw on philosophical arguments like those sprinkled throughout this book. I convince myself that this person's mind is only that much of the Infinite Intelligence that possesses him; that God's thought is always perfect, free from any spot or defect; that this thought of God is the paramount thought in him; and that my conviction concerning this perfection is now falling into Infinite Mind and being brought forward into form.

I may bolster my conviction by recalling desperate cases that I have seen healed through spiritual methods, or that I have heard of or read about. If I am able to determine which *parent thought* is dominant, I select its opposite and weave this belief into my argument with myself. I call up all possible evidences to strengthen my belief in the *master thought* that opposes the *parent thought*.

Talk about the Patient, Not to Him

When I put my treatment into words, I use the third personal pronoun, never the second. I speak *about* the person, not *to* him. Using the pronoun "you" savors of an effort to change his thinking by coercion; perhaps it carries an implication of hypnosis. Using the pronoun "he" indicates my effort to convince *myself* that he is held in the grip of a false belief. When I reach the point where I have formed a picture of the truth about the person, I can then drop my perfect picture into the River of Creative Mind.

I make the treatment apply specifically to the person before me. I use his name. I say, "This is my word spoken for John Smith, living at 1111 Broadway, New York City." I have found this feature effective—not that the Infinite does not know where Smith lives, but the technique gives pinpointedness to my own thought.

Finally, I release the treatment completely and unreservedly to the Infinite. I don't try to help Creative Law bring about the result. I don't push, struggle, or wrestle with it any more than I would try to help keep a planet on its course. My struggling could not possibly help and the tension thereby aroused within me would in itself block the smooth flow of Creative Activity.

Thought Is the Only Treatment

We do not place our hands upon him. Magnetic healers do this; we are not magnetic healers. The only implement we use is spiritual thought.

I do not go out of the way to recommend medicine, surgery, diet or physiotherapy. If the client wishes to avail himself of any or all of these aids, I never try to dissuade him, nor do I refuse to pray for him if he uses them. I believe that the physical and the spiritual method of treating illness are not antagonistic one to the other; they can complement each other. But I leave the physical methods to those expert in these fields. I give *nothing* but prayer treatment coupled with the explanation of what I believe to be the underlying *parent thought*. This enables the person to guard his thought at this particular point.

In more recent years I have asked people for whom I am praying to leave the whole treatment to me. By this I mean that they should not be praying for their own healing during the days or weeks I am doing it. Here is the reason: They are usually so close to their own problem that whenever they think of it they unconsciously tense up, and their tension makes it harder to get through to them. I ask them to quietly say, "I leave myself wide open to every prayer for me that Frederick Bailes utters. I welcome it and its effects." When they are healed, I say: "Now you are on your own. Take over from here. The same Power that has healed you is ready to keep you in excellent health."

Don't Implore, but Declare the Truth

When praying for someone, I do not *ask* that the person shall be healed; I quietly *declare* his perfection. I sometimes allow my imagination to build a picture which helps hold my thought to the healing; I have described some of these useful pictures in other chapters of this book. I find it useful to whisper the words of my prayer treatment; this keeps my thought from wandering.

A businessman told me of his sister, who was suffering from exophthalmic goiter, a systemic toxic condition, in which there is overactivity in the thyroid gland. It is accompanied by a very rapid heartbeat and nerve tremors.

This woman unquestionably "had" the disease. Her heartbeat was rapid, her eyes were bulging, and her hands were in that continuous tremor characteristic of exophthalmic goiter. But a similar rapid heartbeat, trembling hands, and blanched skin of a person terror-stricken by an accident are equally real, although of a temporary nature. As the emotional disturbance subsides the hands, skin, and heart return to normal. So, to minimize the seriousness of his sister's condition in his own mind, he visualized her as just having seen an accident. The woman's complete recovery followed this prayer treatment:

I know that the word I speak for Mrs. Jane Schwelling, 1111 Broadway, New York City, will not return unto me void; it will accomplish that for which it is spoken. Mrs. Schwelling is a complete expression of an Infinite plan, created that Spirit might have another perfect avenue of expression. Her mind is the Mind of the Infinite, quiet, steady, assured. Her body is spiritual substance, being molded at this moment into the form of her thought.

There is no overaction in the Divine Mind. It puts forth just enough effort to carry on all of Its activities. It is never conscious of any need to overact. Its movements are always easily sufficient for the work that must be done. It carries on all of its activities with perfect confidence, easily and effortlessly. It is doing this at this moment in every cell of Mrs. Schwelling's body, and every part of her body knows this and responds to it.

At this moment there is no self-pity in Mrs. Schwelling. She looks out upon a world that is the reflection of her thought about it. She sees all persons as part of the Infinite Creativeness. She fears no one and no thing. She is lifted up far above the slightest twinges of jealousy, she has no anxiety, for she is conscious of one close, inseparable union with the Infinite Healing Presence. Her eyes are open to the truth; the truth is revealing itself to her now.

All of the Power of that Presence is now coursing throughout her body, whether she feels it or not. The chief activity of this Presence is the continuous destruction of everything unlike Itself, and the continuous reproduction in Mrs. Schwelling of that which Infinite Spirit is in Himself.

There is now no obstruction to the free flow of Spirit within her thought. From surface to depths, Spirit thinks through her, and those thoughts are now being reproduced in nerves, thyroid, and every nerve center throughout the entire body. Nothing can operate here but the Law of Right Action.

I give thanks for this before I see it in form, because I release myself and her to the Infinite Creative Mind, knowing that it is now turning these spoken thoughts into form. I accept as a fact the healing of her thought, knowing that it is being manifested in the healing of her body as we release her and it to the only agency in the universe that can turn thoughts into things. And it *is* so.

It will be noticed that healing was not asked for in this prayer, nor were any promises of reformation extended. A treatment is a series of definite statements of the truth about a person, seen as the Infinite sees her. The external condition is ignored except in forming the *master thought* to replace the indicated parent thought.

Samples of Prayer

Here are several samples of prayer illustrating the declaration of truth. I use brief prayers like the following in answer to emergency requests from members of my Sunday congregations.

If the problem is a serious illness, I will say something like this:

Infinite Love now fills this one's mind. Infinite Life

occupies his (her) body. God's healing wisdom streams through every cell in perfect fulfillment.

For someone going into surgery:

The Infinite Knower thinks in one continuous stream of right action through the doctor and through everyone who touches this person.

For the alcoholic:

Infinite Light shines into every recess of this one's mind in a process of self-realization, revealing his complete adequacy to face life without artificial stimulation.

Business situations get:

The never-failing Law is a Law of supply, attracting business to this person's place.

The unemployed are dealt with thus:

This person is God's man (woman) and is always steadily employed in harmonious surroundings at good remuneration.

The person who has just received a verdict of "incurable" is treated thus:

Infinite Life knows no hard nor easy, big nor little, curable nor incurable. Infinite Life now is the most outstanding reality in this person's experience. It flows resistlessly through him (her) in a perfect expression of vitality and wholeness.

What Is God's Truth about Us?

A word of explanation is necessary at this point about the human and the divine views of a person. "Man looketh upon the outward appearance but God looketh on the heart." In our prayer it is necessary that we rise to share God's viewpoint.

We see ourselves and others through the distorted glasses of our poorly developed humanity. We falsely believe that what we see is factual: that man is ill, poverty-stricken, unhappy. But perhaps we do not have the last word in knowledge.

The rock that the scientist of a century ago said was solid substance is now absolutely known to be not solid at all. Yet all the evidence of the senses agreed that the rock was solid. Might it not be that man as he sees himself now is not the real man?

Might it not be that man seen from the other side of the curtain is very different from man seen through our distorted vision? Might it not be that "God looks at the heart" of the matter, and that God sees from the inner side the very opposite of what man sees from the outer appearance?

Man's illnesses could quite easily be nothing more than distorted shadows thrown on the screen of life by distorted thought patterns. Real and painful in his experience, it is not at all beyond the realm of reason to say that if man knew them to be what they truly are he could abolish them.

We should remember that man's spiritual nature is the one remaining unexplored dark continent. The fifteenth-century dweller in the heart of Africa probably never dreamed of vast oceans and continents across the sea. He might well have been exasperated at anyone who tried to tell him that there were races of people with blue eyes and white skins.

The African's common sense told him that he *knew* human beings. He had seen thousands of them, newborn and aged, male and female. But he had never seen a single one with blue eyes and white skin. "If you say there are millions like this, you are going crazy. I'll stick to common sense." The facts were there; but he had never been brought into contact with them.

Much theology is based upon a similarly distorted concept of man. Man has been told that he was conceived in sin and born in iniquity. He has been told that he was created perfect but that his inherent wickedness caused him to "fall," and that this has laid him under God's displeasure. He has been told that illness is God's punishment for his sins, or that it is something to which he must submit.

So long as man held these views, any thorough investigation into the real cause of disease was unthinkable. If we must resign ourselves to the supposed will of a God who lays horrible diseases upon us, then why try to find hidden causes of illness in the thought life?

Man Reproduces the Divine Nature

Our thesis is that man was created to reproduce the divine nature within his character and throughout his body and all of his experiences. The pathway already lies within him; the power to walk that path lies there also. If our assumption is correct, man has the right to be free from *any* limiting experience—whether of body, finances, home, or human relationships.

Spiritual healing would be impossible unless this were so. Man would be left to patch himself up as best he could by the external applications his wit could devise or by internal concoctions that might give him more or less relief from his symptoms. But never could there be the complete and permanent healings that so many millions now experience through the spiritual approach.

It is not easy to treat a person who does not grasp the fundamental principle. These are inclined to the idea that I am some kind of a faith healer with some special gift of healing, which most emphatically I do not have. Those who understand the way the responsive Creative Law operates respond more readily, bearing out the words of the Great Teacher, "Ye shall know the truth and *the truth* shall make you free."

Don't Worry about How It Will Happen

One other important thing to be held in mind by the person using prayer treatment is that he goes *directly to the finished transaction. He does not concern himself with ways and means.* He does not occupy himself with the channels through which the result will come.

In prayer treatment we turn away from the entire outer world. We enter into a silent partnership with Infinite Mind, speak our word for our sick friend or for that one who wishes to put over a business deal, then close with the thought:

Infinite Mind knows a thousand channels that I have never thought of, through which this may come about. If I keep my eyes glued to one keyhole, my good may come in through a door at my back and I shall miss it. It is not my business to work angles, to watch channels. It is my duty to go direct to the Father.

When we watch channels, or try to force them open, we take our eyes off the Creative Agency, which alone can translate our thought into form. We shall be grateful for fulfillment from whatever direction it appears. We weaken our thought by confining attention to any one channel.

Man's duty is to *formulate* the perfect idea, *release* it confidently to Infinite Creativeness, them *leave it alone*. This does not mean that he will not work hard on a sale or try to advertise as convincingly as he can. But he will see these activities merely as the placing of fertilizer around the tree from which he expects apples. The fertilizer is our way of cooperating. The flow of Creative Life from the earth is what eventually puts forth apples.

Don't Let "Incurable" Scare You

In this consideration of channels, means, or possibilities, we also ignore the prognosis of the illness. Frequently, we are told that a famous doctor has said medical science can do nothing for this or that condition. This may be true by all the standards of conscientious medical practice. But we never allow any feeling of hopelessness to enter in at this point; this would be allowing the apparent absence of channels to kill our conviction.

If anything, we dig in deeper at this point. We start at the beginning, recognize that we are dealing with the One Power that built that body years ago. We establish contact with It, knowing that although human aid is impossible, there are still the Infinite resources upon which Creative Law draws. We assert and insist that thousands of others have been healed of this condition through the healing of

176

their false belief, and we release our acceptance of this fact.

We might not know *how* it is to be done. It might be true that necessary structures are now missing from this person's body. But we know that the Infinite Creativeness can bypass deficiencies or obstructions and build whatever channels are necessary for the restoration of normalcy.

One of my colleagues heard of an unlettered working woman who was having great success in praying for the sick. He sought her out: "Just *what* do you do when you give prayer treatment for these people?"

"Well," the simple woman said, "my friends come and tell me what is wrong with them. Then they rattle off a lot of long-sounding words their doctor told them. I never heard of those diseases; so my prayer is: 'O God, I don't know what's wrong with this person but You do; I only know that they're made in Your image and must be perfect, so I'm turning them over to You. From here on You're the whole cheese!'"

Ungraceful language, perhaps. But her treatments had led to hundreds of healings, many of them for persons who had been dismissed by their physicians as incurable. She included that most important segment of prayer, a total and complete release of the person to the Great Physician. She must have had a very high spiritual conviction because her record was good. Throughout history, it has often been the humble person, with little formal education, who has taught God's ways of peace in the heart.

We welcome any channel that opens, but our principal reliance is upon the Infinite Reservoir. Jesus was trying to make this clear to the people when he said, "Yes, I know that you want to be assured of food and raiment, but seek *first* the kingdom of God and His righteousness and you will have these other things." Their eyes were on channels; His was on the Source. This is the divine order of things.

How Long Should a Prayer Treatment Be?

People want to know how long a prayer treatment should be. The answer depends on how long the practitioner must work with himself to rise above all doubt. He should reason with himself until the words he is speaking are backed up by his inward conviction. Sometimes this is done in ten seconds; at other times he must work half an hour to produce this inner assurance. But he *must* bring himself to the point where nothing within him whispers denial of the confident words he speaks in prayer. When that point is reached he should say or think: "This is the true state of the person I'm praying for; it is the most perfect image I can have of him; so I release it to the Creative Law to bring into form."

We arrive at this high point of consciousness first by bringing ourselves into a state of complete relaxation. We try to build an atmosphere of unruffled peace. We may say quietly: "I and the Father are one, even though the Father is greater than I. I partake of His nature. I feel God's tranquillity. I deliberately enter the secret place of the Most High. I lose myself in the sense of God's nearness."

We give support to our faith by quietly declaring: "Thousands have been healed of worse conditions than this one. I know them, have heard of them, or have read of them. I recall Mr. Despond who had been told he had only a few months to live. Now three years later how well he looks! There is no reason why God should not do for this person what he did for Mr. Despond. They both are now being acted upon by Infinite Mind. So I release all hold on Mr. Melancole, knowing the great Creative Process is now going on within his thought and tissues, impelled by the only Healing Power in the universe. I give thanks because Omnipotence is now in charge."

How Often Should One Treat?

The question sometimes comes up, "How many times a day should I pray thus?" As a rule once daily is sufficient; twice a day is ample. This healing is not going to be brought about by our huffing and puffing, by our wrestling in prayer. The only wrestling necessary is with our own doubting consciousness.

When one comes back to this prayer treatment too often during a day, it reveals a glaring lack in his technique. He has not completely *released* it to Infinite Mind. When one gets up from his prayer he should think, "Now, that is out of my hands, and in the best hands in the universe. They will not fail." This is true faith. If the problem persists in coming to mind, one should say, "I'm glad God has it," and go his way.

One should never assume the responsibility for bringing about healing. His responsibility is to call up the clearest concept possible, then release it completely. When one feels that the responsibility for a person's health or his business is in his hands, he is liable to become tense and no prayer given under tension is of any use. It then becomes an expression of his fears rather than of his faith. "The Father that dwelleth in me, *He* doeth the work."

179

Nevertheless, there is one responsibility forever with us. That is to give serious, conscientious prayer treatment whenever it is requested, and never to allow doubts or negative thought to enter regarding that person, no matter how discouraging the situation may look. Ugly conditions can turn into beautiful healings overnight. My observation of beginners in this method has convinced me that they need to be well schooled in the art of looking *through* the frightening condition rather than *at* it.

Sometimes it takes more than one prayer treatment before the results show up. In some instances I have seen weeks or months of prayer before the healing is complete. As a rule, some improvement will be seen within a few days or hours, but we must stay with it until the person is conpletely well.

At this point an important fundamental must be clearly understood. The one praying may find it necessary to continue his daily prayers for an extended period of time. But he must pray each day as if he had never prayed for that person before. Each prayer treatment must be a new, separate transaction in itself. He must come to each prayer as if it were the very first he had ever uttered for that person.

In deciding on a *series* of prayer treatments for a person, there is the danger of mentally envisioning a healing at some date well into the future. But millions of persons have been healed following just *one* prayer. Healing is not a work to be accomplished; it is a revelation. It is the awakening of a person from his nightmare. It is something that can be instantaneous; in fact, one should always look for and expect instantaneous results.

The Only Thing to Heal Is Thought

There is, after all, nothing to be healed but a false belief. This can be done in the twinkling of an eye. The moment it *is* done, the body begins to change. Some external signs of the old thinking may still show, but these will disappear as the new belief works outward. Therefore, repeated treatments merely continue what has been started.

Many years of experience have shown me that there is some sort of cumulative power in repeated prayer treatments. I have not yet convinced myself just how this cumulative effect is produced. It might work the way a child works with a hoop. He gives it the initial thrust, then lightly taps it occasionally to keep it going and to guide it.

Or there might be a different explanation. The person who is praying, like the person for whom he prays, is beset with his own half-blind humanity. Perhaps his prayers carry an admixture of negative thought of which he is not conscious. But one of his prayers may be uttered when he is at a peak of genuine spiritual realization, and this prayer is the one that heals. Just as one sperm out of millions penetrates the ovum, starting the physical creative cycle, so just one prayer will start the spiritual creative cycle.

Whatever the explanation, it has been conclusively demonstrated that repeated prayer is effective.

Will Personal "Unworthiness" Disqualify Your Prayer?

One should never hold back from praying for another out of a sense of guilt or unworthiness. The more conscientious one is, the more vividly aware of his own short-comings he is likely to be.

The fact is that none of us will ever be "good" enough. If healing depended upon the holiness of the practitioner, there would be no healings. Even the person who feels most unworthy should take courage, for perfect healings often come through very imperfect channels. This does not absolve us from trying to live on the highest levels, but it does save us from the inertia coming from overconscientious self-abasement.

We cannot repeat too often that it is *the truth* that heals. Truth sometimes flows through faulty channels. An honest willingness to be used as a healing agent is the chief prerequisite, coupled with an intelligent understanding of what we are trying to do. The Apostle Paul said, "For . . . the Law is spiritual but I am . . . sold under sin." Our faith is in the Creative Law—not in our own real or supposed righteousness.

Ways to Find Assurance of the Power

The ways in which a sense of oneness is induced vary according to the type of individual. Perhaps it could be said that anything that makes the Healing Power vivid or fresh to us is a good method.

We may see the beauty of the setting sun and of the unfolding flower. We may feel the tranquil calm of eventide, observe the ordered march of stars and planets, marvel at the confident swoop of the seagull. We may hear the song of the skylark and watch the loving interchange between a mother and her newborn child.

These are all works of God. From them we can deduce something of the nature of God. We can begin to think God's thoughts after Him. We may know, for example, that the earth, which has been computed to weigh 6,594,126,820,000,000,000,000 tons, is hurled through space at the speed of a rifle bullet, and that this speed never varies; from this we may gain an awareness of the immensity of the Power with which we are dealing.

The Power that holds the universe in control is the selfsame Power that pours Its resources into us and our affairs. Our confidence grows as we come to realize we are dealing with resistless force, force that operates easily, effortlessly, without tugging, wrestling, puffing or panting. This force is not derived from anything physical. It is entirely mental, for It is the Power of the Mind of the Almighty.

Power goes into our word according to the quiet assurance that we engender within ourselves. The less anxiety, the more power. The less struggle and wrestling, the more force released. The less fear of the condition, the greater the spiritual energy released.

I know of a cancer healed because the woman said, "If I had a pimple on my nose, I know it would disappear in a few days, so I wouldn't worry about it. I'm regarding this on my breast as though it were a pimple on my nose. It will disappear."

This simple soul did not know that there is a vast pathological difference between a pimple and a malignancy. But her argument removed her dread fear; this in turn set up whatever healing forces the Law has at its disposal, and her complete healing followed. Someone else copying her formula without her inward conviction might not have been healed.

One man who is eminently successful as a healer said, "I never seemed able to have a deep conviction of the Power. I doubted that I had enough of what it takes to pray effectively. I was going to quit when the thought struck me that I should make my very doubt a matter of prayer."

This was the way he approached it:

I know that millions of people have been healed through scientific prayer, therefore, I know that there must be a Law of Healing. My feelings of doubt are only my own personal idiosyncrasy. They neither prove nor disprove the existence of the Law. My reason is more to be believed than my feelings, therefore, with all my *will* I believe that there is a Law of Healing, and that It operates through *my* word as well as through that of those whom I now envy. I now *will* to believe that my word has power and that my prayers are producing results equal to those of others.

He has since come into national prominence in this field. Few who hear him are aware of his shaky beginnings.

Conviction is most easily achieved when one realizes that he is treating thought by thought, and that one constructive thought is more potent than thousands of destructive thoughts. In healing the body, the only thing to be healed is the thought. The physical manifestation will automatically follow in due course, because the prayer treatment is the expression of truth, and truth removes all obstructions to itself by dissolving out everything that is not truth.

Prayer and the Doctor

It is not necessary to dismiss the doctor. It is no sign of a lack of faith in the Law that one places himself in the care of a physician, especially if the doctor is one who believes that "more things are wrought by prayer than this world dreams of." But if the physician is one who scoffs at the idea of spiritual healing, the patient must fortify himself mentally against the contagion of his physician's thought. Most ill persons are unable to do this. Fortunately, today it is becoming easier to find a physician who is open to the idea of mental and spiritual healing.

During a recent convention of the California Urological Association a well-known Hollywood urologist said that there is a divine power upon which all physicians must ultimately rely in bringing their patients back to health. Long ago another stated, "I treat, but God heals."

And in 1954, Dr. Elmer Hess, president-elect of the American Medical Association, declared:

> A physician who walks into a sick room is not alone. He can only minister to the ailing person with the material tools of medicine—his faith in a Higher Power does the rest. Show me the doctor who denies the existence of the Supreme Being, and I will say that he has no right to practice the healing art. I am afraid, however, that the concentration on basic science in our medical schools is so great that the teaching of spiritual values is almost neglected.

These men did not say that physicians must throw away their valuable training and experience, become lax in diagnosis, or discontinue those measures found necessary to remove obstructions, or rectify physical malformations. They meant that the power that *heals* is more potent than anything that any human can provide. Physicians who recognize this are a blessing to mankind; and they are forerunners of the physicians of the future.

Sometimes the Healing Power begins to act before the physician does. Here is an incident recently reported to me.

A woman was sent to the hospital for radical surgery. One of the nurses, a woman who reads widely, lent her one of my books to read during the three days of preparation for the operation. After two days the woman asked for her clothes. She said she did not need the operation and wanted to go home. The resident physician was called and refused her request. Finally, her husband was sent for. He tried to persuade his wife to go through with the operation. She was adamant in her refusal.

At last her husband said, "Will you come back with me to Dr. X, who sent you in for the operation. If he examines you and says you are healed, you don't have to go through with it. If he says that it is just the same as when he sent you in, will you then come back and have it done?"

"Yes, that's fair. I will agree to that."

They went back for re-examination. Her doctor was amazed. He said, "I certainly know my specialty and I know that you needed that work done a few days ago. But you certainly do not need it now."

Then he remarked on the wonderful manner in which Nature sometimes steps in and corrects serious situations. The woman did not tell him what she had been reading or of her new approach to prayer.

It should be noted that the woman had a definite pathological condition, properly diagnosed by a reputable physician. If it had been just some vague pain or distress, it might easily have been imagined. A functional difficulty might simply have been thrown off. But the condition was neither functional nor imaginary.

How We Cooperate with the Doctor

"Then, there is no need for doctors?"

There will always be a need for doctors. Unfortunately, just as there are occasional physicians who would rather see a patient die than receive healing through spiritual means, so there are believers in spiritual healing who would rather allow the patient to die than see him brought back to health by the skillful ministrations of a physician using material methods. In fact, they will often refuse to pray for anyone who is using material means. One such extremist wrote one of the most ignorant tirades against medical men, which showed a complete lack of understanding of the medical approach, in which he made it appear that doctors, drugs, and devils were one and the same.

The science of medicine has continued to widen its horizons since its inception. The modern physician with his growing knowledge and understanding of the interior structures and forces of the body, the activity of its glands, the effects of thought upon structure and function, and with his progressively more exact methods of diagnosis, is a distinct benefactor to the human race. There is still a need for skillful surgery, and the growing number of wonder drugs and serums fills a distinct need in the community.

As long as men engage in destructive emotions, there will be need for physicians. Man is a long time emerging into the clear light of his spiritual nature. His emotional tangles will produce enough physical disorders to keep physicians busy for the immediate future. But the alert physician is looking more and more deeply into the thought life of his patient. He will do this increasingly as the centuries roll on.

It is a fact that physical and spiritual methods of healing are not separate and antagonistic. They are merely two ends of the same stick. Like two pillars, they may seem to stand stiffly separate as though to say, "Never we twain shall meet," but somewhere in the vault of heaven they form an arch.

Our investigation into the Power that heals frees us from many of the superstitions and exaggerations of the past. The doctor's scientific discipline helps reveal to us a divine Power that is not denominational. When a physician speaks of a divine Power, he does not necessarily picture priest, ritual, or creed, nor does he envision a wrathful God Who must be appeased. He thinks of an intelligent Person working through an Intelligent Universal Principle equally distributed throughout the world of nature, including man.

We cooperate with the physician in this way. If praying for one who is under medical or surgical treatment, we quietly declare that there is only One Mind in the universe. This Mind flows steadily through that doctor as he examines the patient or reads an X-ray plate. It is the One Perfect Knower. While It can heal directly through the thought, It can operate also through any material means that tends in the direction of repair or restoration or normalcy. The Mind thinks through the brain and fingers of every person who has anything to do with the person for whom we are praying.

In surgery, we use a prayer treatment such as the following:

I know that Jacob Jacobsen is forever indwelt and surrounded by the Infinite Mind which always is working to bring right action into him. This Mind operates also as the mind of every surgeon, anaesthetist, nurse, and assistant who has anything to do with Jacob Jacobsen. Each becomes the assistant to the One Great Physician, Who thinks through each one, so that each one is impelled to do exactly the right thing at the right time. No mistakes are made; none can be made. Each thinks with clear discrimination, steadiness, and poise. One perfect circle of right action surrounds Jacob Jacobsen and his environment.

The Great Physician thinks through the thought of Jacob Jacobsen, so that the healing currents of life flow steadily through him. His recovery is assured. Healing moves easily and rapidly in all of his tissues, starting in the depths of his buried mind, rising to the surface, extending through every cell of his body. I now release Jacob Jacobsen and everyone who touches him to be unconsciously guided by the Great Knower. This is the truth about him, and it *is* so.

It has become a commonplace to have people tell us the doctor has been happily surprised at their rapid recovery. The physician himself has sometimes told us that, for some unaccountable reason, he felt impelled to change his approach or his techniques during an operation, and the outcome proved it to have been a most intelligent move. Sometimes "God moves in mysterious ways, His wonders to perform."

chapter thirteen

Helpful Techniques

in Prayer Treatment

DURING THE PAST QUARTER CENTURY I HAVE WORKED OUT
various techniques to help me set the Healing Law in motion. My colleagues and students whom I have trained have
developed approaches that are helpful to them. The reader
of this book will undoubtedly discover points of practice
that will suit his own temperament. In this chapter I shall
describe several techniques that have proved effective.

The "Fog" Method

Each Sunday I use the "fog" method just before going
out on the platform to greet the congregation. I remain
silent for a few minutes while I allow my thought to rest
upon the picture of the Infinite Healing Presence slowly
filling the entire building.

I picture a luminous fog drifting in through doors and

windows, silently filling and saturating every seat, spreading all the way back to the topmost balcony, enveloping every chandelier, the organ, the stage, the curtains, the speaker, and penetrating the body of each person to its inmost center.

All of us think in pictures. Our words are only our descriptions of pictures constantly flitting through our brains. Someone has said that one picture is worth a thousand words. This is doubly true in praying.

I have lived near various coasts. The silence with which a fog drifts in, the thoroughness with which it saturates everything, its unfelt movement as it quietly takes its place, all combine to give me a feeling of the resistless movement of the Infinite Healing Presence. Whether It acts like this does not matter; what does matter is that I find in the fog a way of visualizing an abstract idea. The fact that so many receive healing each Sunday has shown me the value of this technique.

The "Fog" Method Heals a Brain Tumor

This "fog" method of treatment is far from "foggy." Its effect may be quite specific and pinpointed. It was chosen, for example, by one of my colleagues for use on a young man who had "inoperable malignant tumor of the brain." The diagnosis was based on hospital tests and X-rays; the patient was told he had only a few months to live.

Very often the spiritual practitioner gets the hopeless cases. After everything else has been tried, they think they might as well try us. Someone once said, "They send for the spiritual practitioner and the undertaker at the same time, and whoever gets there first gets the case."

This young man's situation was approached as follows: The alarming prognosis of incurability was ignored. The only reality admitted was that of the Infinite Healing Presence operating through resistless Law.

The seriousness of the condition was never again spoken of to anyone connected with him. This is important. Hospitals are fine places, but patients get together and discuss the seriousness of their problems. Friends call; the talk sooner or later gets around to the menacing predictions. The result is that the general atmosphere is not that of optimism.

This young man was seen, not as a physical body, but as a mind. His body was seen only as the flesh shadow thrown by the invisible Thinker, Himself. The body was seen as a creation of Spirit; the spiritual substance of the body could be restored to its original perfect pattern once the interference of distorting thought patterns was removed.

Now for the fog. The young man's entire atmosphere was seen to be a spiritual presence, soaking and saturating everything in his home, his room, his clothes, his body. Nothing could escape it. Silently, without force, struggle, or wrestling, it moved in until the body faded out of the picture and a new one, composed of the substance of Spirit, took its place. The quiet declaration was made that no part of the house, the furnishings, or his body could escape the steady infiltration of the Infinite Healing Presence. Nor did it wish to escape It; it welcomed It.

His complete inward peace of mind was made the center of the prayer treatment. He was seen as one resting in the soft arms of the Creative Law "as the earth lies in the soft arms of the atmosphere." Peace was declared to be the law of his life; his mind was declared to be one with the Infinite Mind, therefore free of any ugly distortion.

Within four months, he was re-examined and X-rayed again. Not the slightest trace of tumor was found. Today, almost five years later, he is an active, happy member of society.

A "Fog" Prayer Treatment

Prayer treatment for him took approximately the following form:

> Consciousness is the prime reality, the consciousness of God and the consciousness of John Cerebra for whom this treatment is being given. All outward conditions are nothing but the projections of his consciousness; they have no more abiding reality than the image thrown on a motion-picture screen.
>
> This word that I speak is the Power and Presence of the Infinite. It has the power to set Law in motion—to change the reel in the projection booth—so that a different image is thrown on the outer screen of John Cerebra's experience.
>
> The Infinite Healing Law is now gently stealing into action at every point around him and within him. It fills all space, the atmosphere of the city, the home, the room in which he happens to be at this moment. It penetrates to his innermost cell and into every cell. It saturates his brain, and its effect is a quiet, unruffled peace of mind.
>
> Not *some* of the power but *all* of the power of God

is concentrated at the central point of his inner consciousness, transforming it into a God-consciousness, and reproducing its own quiet assurance within John Cerebra. Peace is the Law of his life.

This peace is even now reflecting itself in every cell of his body. The Law of Life is greater than the Law of Death; the Law of Perfection is greater than any Law of Imperfection. The Law of the Spirit of Life in the Christ is now setting him free from the Law of Sin and Death.

We release John Cerebra unequivocally and unreservedly to the Law of the Spirit of Life, giving thanks for its perfect work in him. And it *is* so.

The vivid picture of the surrounding and penetrating Healing Mist of Infinite Creative Law was given paramount reality in treating John Cerebra. Of course we knew that It always *was* there. Seeing It as stealing into and through the patient was only a device made necessary by the limitations of our humanity.

The "Invisible-Wave" Method

Akin to the "fog" method is a somewhat similar device, the "invisible-wave" method. After the practitioner has induced a state of peace within his own mind, by dwelling upon all that he believes the Mind of God to be in Its essence, he draws upon one of the latest discoveries in physical science.

Today the hardest steel is being cut by means of sound waves. A mechanic can direct these sound waves at a particular point on a steel plate, and they cut right through. He can cut squares, circles, and other geometrical forms with the exactness with which one could cut paper with a razor blade. He can also cut ragged holes as with a fretsaw. Yet this is all done with sound waves that man's ears cannot pick up. It seems that the mechanic is pointing a tool without a blade and that the object is cut merely by being pointed at.

We *know*, however, that the cutting is done by a terrific concentration of sound waves turned in a specific direction to accomplish a specific result. X-rays are sometimes used in this way against tumors. The practitioner keeps this in mind while giving an "invisible-wave" prayer treatment.

A certain type of mind finds it difficult to confine thought to the abstract. The person must have some tangible object or a specific picture in which to center his thought. So he thinks of the Infinite Healing Power as similar to these invisible sound waves. His prayer treatment is the tool that he points at the *parent thought* underlying the condition.

The practitioner using this idea may be diverted into directing his attention and treatment toward the physical condition instead of the *parent thought*. This I have warned against previously. To avert this mistake, the practitioner should tell himself:

> The only healer is the Spirit of God; the only thing to be healed is John Cerebra's thought. The thought of God is now becoming the thought of John Cerebra. It is now concentrating itself at the exact spot in his mind where the distortion arises, flowing through that to transform it, then flowing through the distorted manifestation to destroy that by its pinpointed concentration at that point.

The "Invisible-Wave" Method in Obscure Cases

When the cause or the location of the trouble is unknown, this penetrative "invisible-wave" method is valuable. The practitioner confidently affirms that the Infinite Knower knows exactly where the difficulty originates, and pours Himself through the body with more than enough force to shatter the blockage at whatever point it originates.

One certainly takes cognizance of the physical or financial condition to be healed, when it is known; otherwise the prayer could not have the specificity that we insist on. The art of successful praying consists in giving the inner thought and the outer condition the proper ratio of attention.

Thus, probably 90 per cent of our attention is on the basic thought distortion and 10 per cent on the distortion in the outer life. The prayer treatment is out of balance when these percentages are reversed. As explained before, we ascertain the outer condition to be healed, determine the destructive *parent thought* that gave rise to it, then introduce the *master thought*, and treat to induce a changed thought pattern. The newly induced thought looks toward the external problem, which is the manifestation of the former destructive thought, and declares the manifestation is changing to be in harmony with the changed thought.

The "Contracting-Expanding" Method

I sometimes use what might be called a "contracting-expanding" method of praying. In this method, after hav-

ing induced within myself as complete a sense of tranquillity as possible, I call up a picture of a gigantic circle.
I make this circle as large as possible, sufficient to encom-
pass the farthest star. Then, in my mind's eye, I see it
swiftly contracting to encircle only the solar system, then
the atmosphere surrounding the earth, then the country in
which the person is, then the city in which he lives, then
his house, then himself. I see it drawing to a tiny circle
surrounding the innermost cell of his body.

This circle to me represents the Infinite Healing Law.
My thought has now drawn It into the center of the person's body, his business, his home, or wherever the trouble
is located. When It has assumed a vivid reality to me, I
then try to see It start to expand. I have made Its con-
traction a swift operation; I make Its expansion a slower
process. I see It slowly, steadily widening Itself until It
fills that inmost cell, then spreading through the organ
involved, through the entire system, missing nothing, expanding Itself and Its perfect action gradually outward
until It fills every cell of the body including the skin.

Here it stays. At this point, I quietly declare that It
is the only Reality in the person and his affairs; that this
concept now dominates his thought. It is the one Law that
includes within Itself all lesser (material) laws. Nothing is
difficult, nothing incurable, nothing hopeless to It. It is
all of the Power of Infinite God. It dominates the person's
thought; it is the motive Power of every function of his
body. It is the Alpha and the Omega, the beginning and
the end.

At this point I drop out of the picture, turning everything over to It. My part has been only to see the troubled person as he really is, played upon by the Infinite Healing Presence. As I release him to this Healing Principle, my responsibility ends. God is the Healer, not I.

This has proved to be a most effective method of treatment. I have seen many persons pronounced incurable brought back into excellent health through the use of this technique. It came to me suddenly one day while reading that verse, "He must increase, but I must decrease."

The Importance of Spiritual Awareness

It is necessary that we recognize the difference between an intellectual *assent* and a spiritual *awareness*. The mere following of a technique will often produce fine results, but in order to succeed consistently one must come to the stage of awareness. He must realize an inner conviction.

In the use of any of the methods described in this chapter the results will improve as the user's inward awareness improves. If the picture of the contracting-expanding circle, for example, is accompanied by a vivid awareness of the Infinite Healing Presence actually in action, it will then be more than a technique; it will be a living reality. The practitioner will be a conscious co-worker with God.

Growing out of this will be a sense of freedom. The entire responsibility for the healing will not be the practitioner's, but God's. As he releases his picture of the expanding circle, he will not be strained and apprehensive. His power will not rest on his personal ability; it will be based upon the fact that the Infinite Creative Law rushes in to heal at any point at which it is properly approached. His part is simply to build any picture that helps him realize intelligently what he is doing.

The Power of the Quiet Mind

The word "quiet" or "quietly" is often used in this book. Quietness is the proper mood of prayer. Jesus said, "They think that they shall be heard for their much speaking (shouting and straining)."

A very human tendency is to think things must be accomplished by "blood, sweat and tears." We imagine that unless we wrestle with a prayer we are not doing our share, not showing our intense desire for its answer. We labor under the false notion that the raised voice, the gritted teeth, show our sincerity.

Quite the contrary is true. Strength in prayer comes from quiet acceptance of the fact that the Great Physician is at work. The practitioner has merely ushered God into the room where the sick person lies. Here his responsibility ends. A shrieking receptionist would hinder, not help.

A rabble-rouser might gain a crowd by his sweating vehemence; a spiritual practitioner gains strength through quietness. "In quietness and in confidence shall be your strength."

The "Authoritative" Method

A former professional boxer, a man of splendid physical inheritance and high intelligence, came to see me. He said, "I've been losing weight for several months, but no one can find out what's the matter with me. I've been X-rayed; I've had basal-metabolism tests, blood-chemistry tests, and a host of other tests. There seems to be nothing physically to hang this thing on. But I have splitting headaches, have no strength, no appetite. At first they thought it must be cancer, but there's no sign of that. Now they think that it is either a glandular trouble, or else something in my subconscious mind.

"Something you said on the air gave me hope that you might help me. Maybe you can show me what's wrong with my thinking. I've tried, but there's nothing I can trace the trouble to. I'm happily married; I've had a good job ever since I quit boxing; and my wife says I've never shown signs of being neurotic."

I told him that I had seen similar conditions. To search and probe for their cause usually made the sufferer worse, because his spirits sank after each unsuccessful probing. But I knew of one method he could follow that might well clear up the trouble.

I said, "Suppose a delivery man from a department store knocks at your door. He holds a box in which there is, let us say, a girdle. He says there is a fifteen-dollar C.O.D.

"You tell him that you did not order it. You check with your wife; she didn't order it. So you refuse it.

"But the man persists. It has your name and address on it. It must be for you. He annoys you by his insistence. All your arguments fail to move him. You cannot imagine how this unwanted thing was brought to your door. All you know is that you don't want it.

"You have recourse to one thing. The law says that you need not accept delivery of anything that you have not ordered. Therefore, you say, 'I don't know how, why, or where your company got the notion that I want a girdle. I never ordered one. *I refuse to accept it.*' And you firmly close the door in his face. He cannot force it upon you without your consent. This is the law.

"Since in your illness skilled investigators have been unable to find the cause, either in your body or in your thought life, it is evident that you cannot treat the specific thought away. Ordinarily we trace back from the condition to the thought, and treat the thought rather than the condition. In this instance we cannot find the thought; so we must reverse the procedure. We must, in a sense, attack the condition directly. We can do this working along the following line of thought:

> This condition is one not definitely sought by me. I do not like it, want it, enjoy it, or welcome it. My body does not wish it, and I simply will not have it. I refuse to accept it, knowing that I do not have to accept anything that I did not ask for. I am a thinker; therefore, my thought is superior to the physical manifestation. As a thinker, I am able to 'decree a thing and it shall be established unto me.' I now very definitely order it out along with whatever gave it birth. I very definitely refuse it and shut the door of my mental life upon it now and forever.

"Affirm this whenever you think of your trouble. Do it very specifically three times daily. Assume a position in which you are as superior to it as you were to that delivery man. You knew that you could have thrown him out physically if he had not obeyed your order to take the girdle away. Assume that same superman feeling toward this, whatever it is.

"This thing has you worried because no one seems

202

able to tell you what it is or what is causing it. Worry is fear. Do what you can to rise above that fear. It has been commanding you; now you start to command it."

About a week later he telephoned and said, "Before my fight with Joe Doe a few years ago, I was worried. He was a terrific hitter and I couldn't help hoping he wouldn't put me down. While training for him, I would sometimes think of being knocked out. I would hope that the back of my head would not strike hard and do serious injury. I worried what would happen to my wife and kids if I was incapacitated for work.

"My manager sensed this and said, 'Listen Bill, you're letting this guy get the Indian sign on you. You're going to beat yourself before you get in there with him. Now look at it sensibly. You're plenty fast and you don't make mistakes; you can stay out of the way of his right hand. And you're a good clouter yourself. Don't worry about him; let *him* worry about you.'

"So I took the play away from Joe. I made him fight me the way I wanted him to; and I put him away in the third round.

"I've been reliving those weeks these past few days. I've done the same kind of thinking I did then. I've got the quiet confidence that I'm making this thing fight *my* way, and I feel a thousand per cent better."

To this day Bill does not know where the trouble lay, nor do I. But he is well and happy.

Bill's case is a good example of the "authoritative method" of treatment. Jesus seems to have used it frequently in what was called the casting out of "devils." He used it in the temptation in the wilderness.

Nothing Comes without Our Consent

Nothing can ever come into our lives but that which we either consciously or unconsciously ask for. Even if we cannot trace our way back to the unconscious wish, we can still reverse that wish. We can declare that we did not want this condition and that we absolutely refuse to accept it.

We should not be too greatly concerned because we cannot discover which particular wish caused the condition. Our refusal to accept it, saying that we do not need nor want it, constitutes a reversal. In one sense we have worked on the effect to change the cause, which is the opposite of our usual method. But the treatment does tie the visible condition to its unseen cause, and negates it at its source.

The "Convergent" Method

A woman had been confined to a wheel chair by arthritis. She was of a singularly gracious disposition in her dealings with others, but her face in repose fell into lines which could be described as tight, if not harsh. This might be ascribed to continuous pain; yet it might also evidence a buried resentment, which is often the hidden mental foundation for arthritis.

Discussion brought out the fact that in her college days she had wanted to become a missionary to Africa. Her wealthy parents had absolutely forbidden this. She had given in after she had seen that they were adamant, but resentment had smoldered within her. She had married, but on their honeymoon in Europe their chauffeur had been secretly drinking, and there was an accident. Her bridegroom was instantly killed and she was thrown into a state of severe shock, although her physical injuries were not serious.

This was the second time that life had closed the gate of happiness. Her resentment was growing.

Eventually, she inherited her parents' wealth and plunged into a determinedly gay social whirl. She had a few quite unsatisfactory sexual experiences, after which she turned her back upon society, gave up all thought of finding happiness in love, and began to use her money in helping distressed families. But inwardly she nourished a resentment toward men.

Through faulty investment counsel, she lost most of her fortune and became a dress saleswoman. Resentment now was a storm raging within her and it had broadened to include God, Who she thought had laid this crowning indignity upon her.

Now arthritis touched her with its crippling hand. Her early training enabled her to maintain an outward graciousness but, upon questioning, she admitted that she was most resentful at what life, God, and people had done to her.

"But," she wept, "what am I to do? I've tried my hardest to get rid of this hidden resentment. I was trained from childhood to be a lady outwardly, but no one ever showed me how to free myself from these inward ugli-nesses."

She had superlative will power, as many arthritics have. She said, "Just tell me what to do and I'll stick to it if it kills me."

I replied, "This is one place where your will power is better left outside the door. I believe that you can be helped if you will allow yourself to become passive. Stop thinking of the brave fight *you* will wage. Instead, let yourself be played upon by something that acts from outside yourself."

At this point I might point out a crucial difference between the excellent methods of the psychologist and those of the spiritual practitioner. Both of these try to induce a changed belief in the distressed person. But the psychologist places the pivotal point of power within the person himself; it must be *his* faith in *his own* power to change his life. On the contrary, the spiritual practitioner believes that faith to be effective must start with God. This woman's belief in herself had not emancipated her; in fact it had brought her to this sorry pass. A vastly superior Power was now needed to bring her out of her defeat.

I said, "You have been having infrared therapy. Your will power did not enter in there. You lay there completely surrendered to the flow of those heat waves. Suppose we use them as an illustration of what is taking place; only we shall spiritualize them."

I prayed for her there in the office and told her I would do the same thing daily for as many weeks as seemed necessary while she was in her own home. The prayer treatment went something like this:

> Mrs. Laidy's condition is the result of her resentments, perhaps coupled with the emotional shock of the accident in France years ago. But *her resentments are all mistaken beliefs.* Her parents loved her and worked constantly to ensure her happiness. Men she encountered had

good reasons for not going into marriage with her. The accident was not preordained of God; it was the result of the chauffeur's carelessness. Her fortune was diminished by unsound advice; it would have been increased by a wiser selection of counselor. God did not single her out for impoverishment nor for arthritis. These were the inescapable effects of wrong causes.

At this moment, *Mrs. Laidy is surrendered to the flow of Infinite healing currents*, just as real and infinitely more potent than the infrared rays. They stream endlessly from each of the four corners of the ceiling above us. They converge upon her, meeting exactly at her location, following her wherever she goes when she leaves the room, and always focused upon her, as a spotlight follows a performer.

They *penetrate to the deepest levels of her deeper mind*. They are now setting up their own perfect vibration in her depths, forcing the irregular discordant waves of her resentment to coincide with their harmonies. She does not struggle to check resentment. She allows the spiritual infrared of the Healing Presence to blot them out.

This *Infinite Creative Process* is now at work in her physical body. It *knows the chemical processes* by which the deposits in her joints can be dissolved and carried to their rightful place in other parts of her body. It wants her to be a free channel for Its expression. It wants her to be able to perform her duties easily and gracefully. It is now removing all that would block that perfect freedom.

It *remains converged upon her* from every angle, following her in the store, the bus, the automobile, and focusing upon her as she sleeps.

A new love for people is awakening within her. She

makes allowances for those who she thought had wronged her. She pities everyone whose blindness makes him hurt others. The beauty of life, and the inner beauty of those with ugly exteriors, fill her soul and express through every joint, in gladness, freedom, flexibility.

She remains passive to this play of Infinite Life and Wisdom upon her. Not through her effort but through *the play of God upon and through her*, her outlook upon life is healed, and her body reflects this inward healing. And it *is* so.

I would like to say that all traces of her former trouble have disappeared. They have not; there are a few knobby places left. But she is no longer crippled. It is quite likely that even the last signs of her former bondage will disappear. She is still a charming person outwardly, but better still, she now has an inner tranquillity which she had never known. Now that she is poor, she is richer than when she was rich, for *she is physically free to live life as she wants to.*

This "convergent" method of prayer treatment makes the healing a distinctly personal affair. It is as if God has left the running of the universe to subordinates while He concentrates upon a single person.

Our finite minds find it difficult to grasp the Infinite resourcefulness. Of course we know that God does not have to turn anything over to subordinates. God is that circle whose circumference is nowhere and whose center is everywhere. He is building millions of new unborn bodies at this moment and healing thousands who are placing themselves in as passive a condition to Him as are the unborn; all this without any division of His attention.

"How Much Can Happen through Me?"

Results are produced at the level of our belief. No one can expect results one millimeter higher than his faith. *Our ability to conceive of something as happening through us becomes the measure of our accomplishment.*

The boundary of our manifestation is not advanced by our wishes, hopes, or pleas. The advance is made by our spoken *declaration*, backed up by our inward *conviction*. Results will follow to the extent of our belief in God's willingness and ability to work through us.

Here are five questions we must answer correctly before our prayers will work.

First. Is the Infinite *willing* that this person's peace of mind shall be restored? To this, an unqualified yes. Is He *able?* Again, yes. Have others been healed? A million times yes.

Second. Were the persons who were healed arbitrarily selected? No. Were they of a fortunate disposition especially susceptible to healing or to suggestion? No. Some were trained in the methods of scientific skepticism.

Third. How far does the healing depend on me? It depends chiefly on my getting myself out of the way and allowing Infinite Creativeness to flow unobstructedly. It flows freely where there is no discordant thought in me. Where there is an inner awareness of peace, assurance, love, understanding, and confidence, It goes into action. It is obstructed by envy, anxiety, worry, hatred, jealousy, resentment, or any desire to separate anyone else from his good. I get *myself* out of the way when I cultivate the Godlike qualities.

Fourth. Just exactly *what* brings about the healing? *The desire of Spirit to fulfill Itself in the organism It has created produces the healing.* It reproduces Itself and Its own qualities in that which It has brought into being. Its tendency is to flow through without being invited. *The sole purpose of prayer treatment is to remove the barriers of thought that hinder the flow of Spirit.*

Fifth. And perhaps the most important. In just what does my faith lie, or upon what does it rest? Millions have what they call "faith," but it does not heal them. It is a belief in a creed or a system of theology, detached from their practical problems. It might make them acceptable church members, but in their personal affairs it is totally useless.

Fortunately, many devoted church believers have had a glorious *working* faith in addition to their creedal beliefs. They have learned how to apply spiritual principles to practical affairs, even while others were keeping their religious faith a thing apart from daily living.

Let us take a look at a true workable faith. The faith that heals is threefold.

It is first a belief that *our deep-lying mental and emotional patterns determine the shape and color of our outer experience.* Unless one believes this, he will always be looking in the wrong direction for the cause of his unhappiness.

No one is a failure simply because he falls. He becomes a failure when he says that someone pushed him down. He who has the right kind of belief always looks within himself for the cause of his illness, failure, or unhappiness. This is fundamental.

The second leg of a person's dynamic belief is his *awareness of the inexorable steady thrust of the Creative Law, always following the direction of his deep mental states.* His part is to supply the mental pattern; God's part is to work out the pattern into form. This is always the divine sequence; it always has been so; it will never change. But a person must accept it, believe it, rest upon it, release himself to it.

The third leg of this tripod upon which faith rests is *a determination never willingly to hurt another.* I deal elsewhere with the reasons for this. Harsh, cruel, or tricky treatment of others kills the power of spiritual prayer treatment. In fact, as one develops his spiritual awareness, he will find that he loses even the desire to criticize others, to pass on unpleasant gossip he has heard, or to belittle anyone.

Jesus was faced daily by men who preened themselves on the fact that they were orthodox. They fulfilled every requirement of the religious law; their theology was scrupulously correct. Their prayers were verbally faultless. They could become frenzied debating some obscure point of theological law.

But Jesus sensed that all of these things were external to them. They discussed words but missed spiritual meanings. He detected a lack at one vital point.

This vital spot was all-important. They lacked the spirit of love.

Christ knew the value of good theology. He was aware of the need for proper observance of form and ritual. He observed all of these externals himself. But he knew that the externals were only for the purpose of expressing the heart of religion, which was *love*.

The Healing Law Is the Law of Love

Jesus never uttered a word unless it had profound meaning. He cut to the heart and intent of all religion when he said, "Therefore, all things whatsover ye would that men should do to you, do ye even so to them; for this is the law and the prophets." Paul simplified the same idea, by saying, "Love is the fulfilling of the law."

The law is fulfilled only through love. Paul elaborated upon this fundamental when he said, in the beautiful thirteenth chapter of First Corinthians: "Though I speak with the tongues of men and of angels and have not love, I am become as sounding brass or a tinkling cymbal. And though I have all knowledge and have not love, I am nothing. Love is kind. Love vaunteth not itself, is not puffed up. Love is not easily provoked, thinketh no evil. The greatest . . . is love."

Love is the most potent healing force in the universe. It heals him who gives it and him who receives it. The loving heart is compassionate toward those whom life has made disagreeable and unlovable. Its understanding sees why they act as they do. It pushes its own hurt feelings into the background, refuses to take offense. It pours itself into the suffering, even into the meanness of others by rising above all self-centered resentment.

The loving heart cannot be hurt, for it transcends all egoism. It is lifted upon the gentle love currents of the Infinite as a glider is wafted aloft on the air currents. From this exalted vantage point, it sees things fall into proper perspective. It sees motives as well as actions. It knows that the disagreeable person lashes out at whoever is near, but is in reality blindly lashing out at life or at himself.

Anyone Can Cultivate Love

The loving heart is always the understanding heart. "Love suffereth long, and is *kind*." If we doubt that we have the true spirit of love, we can at least be kind. This in itself tends to engender the genuine inward loving necessary to healing, for "feeling follows action," and we tend to become like our actions.

This then is the faith that moves mountains. It rests upon the tripod of knowledge, trust, and love. It will tumble if one of the three is lacking. The encouraging thing is that when each is assiduously cultivated, you have become a highly efficient, praying person. You can heal yourself and others. It is that simple.

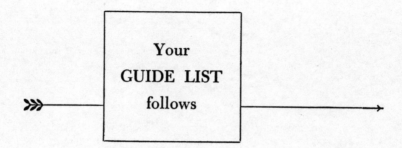

Guide-List for Overcoming

Specific Problems

IT WOULD TAKE VOLUMES TO GO INTO DETAIL CONCERNING all of the conditions growing out of the different parent thoughts.

However, appended is a list of the experiences that I have found to be commonly connected with various parent thoughts.

I have given the corrective master thought for each group of troubles.

I have deliberately made the prayer treatments brief so that you may add a sentence or two of your own words. That way, you will invest them with something of your own consciousness and avoid the danger of merely repeating my words.

It must always be remembered that the change in one's circumstances lies in more than the correction of the inner thought pattern. It lies in the flow of divine force through the changed belief. The latter is necessary only to clear the way for this Infinite Power to act.

Parent Thought		Master Thought
OVERLOAD, FUTILITY		ADEQUACY, RESOURCEFULNESS
"I can't go through with this!"	*The thought in words*	"My strength is sufficient for thee."

SOME OF THE PROBLEMS BORN FROM THE PARENT THOUGHT	
alcoholism	high blood pressure
anemia	inferiority complex
anxiety	insanity
haste (undue, leading to blunders)	nervous breakdown
	overweight
hatred of those who succeed	paralysis
heart (palpitation)	

PRAYER TREATMENT FOR THE ABOVE PROBLEMS

God has never seen anything from which He need shrink or run away, for He is Supreme Mind. I also am mind inhabiting body. Since I am an extension of Infinite Mind, I can easily carry any load. I am adequate to face life at any point. I refuse to allow traitorous thoughts to sneak into the citadel of my thinking. I invite all the resourcefulness and the resources of the Infinite to take over my defense now and throughout the coming years.

(Add a sentence or two of your own)_____

_____

_____

_____

Parent Thought **LOSS** ——— "My loss, my loss, my loss!"	*The thought in words*	Master Thought **INSEPARABLE ONENESS** ——— "Nothing is ever lost in the Infinite Mind."

**SOME OF THE PROBLEMS BORN FROM
THE PARENT THOUGHT**

loss of organ function or sanity
loss of property, job, business, customers, sales
loss of reputation, love, beauty, youthfulness
loss of loved ones, friends

PRAYER TREATMENT FOR THE
ABOVE PROBLEMS

Nothing is ever lost to the Divine Mind. The Knower in me already knows where this desired thing is. It knows where I am. It brings me to it, or it to me. It throws light so that I can know how to be reunited with that which appears to be lost. I refuse to accept the idea of loss at any point, anywhere in my experience. I believe in union; therefore, everything in my life is always in its right place.

(Add a sentence or two of your own)_____

_____

_____

_____

_____

_____

Parent Thought		Master Thought
OBSTRUCTION, DELAY		RESISTLESSNESS
"This person, place, thing opposes or blocks me; refuses to budge."	*The thought in words*	"Nothing can stand in the way of the resistless flow of the Infinite expression."

SOME OF THE PROBLEMS BORN FROM THE PARENT THOUGHT

cataract	embolism
circulation	getting loans
closing of sales	getting a raise
constipation	hardening of arteries
coronary occlusion	promotion in business
deafness	sale of property
delay in love and marriage	

PRAYER TREATMENT FOR THE ABOVE PROBLEMS

The obstacles I seem to see in the outer world all arise within myself in my false belief about myself and the universe. I rest in the assurance that what I desire is only the out-thrust of the Infinite in me seeking fuller expression.

God sees nothing that wishes to obstruct Him or that would be able to. I range myself alongside Him and fill my consciousness with the assurance of the resistless flow of the Infinite Will through me.

(Add a sentence or two of your own)_____

_____

Parent Thought		Master Thought
IRRITATION		TRANQUILITY
"Things irritate me."	*The thought in words*	"Nothing outside of me has the power to irritate me without my consent."

SOME OF THE PROBLEMS BORN
OF THE PARENT THOUGHT

eczema and all skin irritations
all physical conditions ending in "itis" which means inflammation
ulcers, shingles, catarrh, sinus trouble, gall bladder trouble
hypersensitiveness to criticism
intolerance of people who are "different"

PRAYER TREATMENT FOR THE
ABOVE PROBLEMS

There is a world within me that is completely free from any sense of irritation. It is the secret place of the Most High, where tranquility reigns supreme. Nothing can enter here without my consent. I refuse to allow it to be disturbed by any intruder. My mind is cool in the face of a thousand aggravations. God thinks his peace through me.

(Add a sentence or two of your own)_____

_____

_____

_____

_____

_____

Parent Thought		Master Thought
HOSTILITY, CROSS-PURPOSES	*The thought in words*	**NO COMPETITION**
———		———
"People are against me."		"The world is friendly."

SOME OF THE PROBLEMS BORN FROM THE PARENT THOUGHT

allergies, hay fever, migraine, virus
amoebic infections, bacterial infections
asthma (in children often due to hostility between parents)
unexplainable hostility of others toward us
uncooperativeness
boils, leukemia, malignancy
jealousy, war, gossip, criticism

PRAYER TREATMENT FOR THE ABOVE PROBLEMS

I am one cell in the body of God. Basically, there can be no real enmity between me and any other cell. There can be no angry competition between us, because each of us is always working for the other, consciously or unconsciously.

I carry the feeling of forgiveness toward anyone who has wronged me. I refuse to entertain suspicion toward those who have not wronged me. I cultivate the expectancy of good in all people, and I draw from them the same feelings.

(Add a sentence or two of your own)_____

_____

_____

_____

Parent Thought		Master Thought
REJECTION	*The thought*	SELF-APPRECIATION
"People look down on me, or don't want me."	*in words*	"I know my true worth."

**SOME OF THE PROBLEMS BORN FROM
THE PARENT THOUGHT**

dislocations, fractures, detached retina

failure in business, failure to attract love or friends

hesitancy, bashfulness, jiltings, suppressed rage, self-depreciation

difficulty in finding the right work, misunderstanding by others

---

PRAYER TREATMENT FOR THE
ABOVE PROBLEMS

There is only one Good. I am united with this Good, at every point. I am a better, wiser, stronger, more attractive person than I have allowed myself to believe.

I have belittled myself, undervalued myself. Others may have caught this thought atmosphere about me.

Henceforth they will catch the new atmosphere, because I know my true worth. Every part of me is strongly united to every other part and to God, in mind, body, and character.

(Add a sentence or two of your own)_____

_____

_____

_____

223

Parent Thought		Master Thought
WRONG ACTION	*The thought*	**RIGHT ACTION**
"Illness, trouble are natural."	*in words*	"Health and joy are natural."

> ANY AND ALL KINDS OF PROBLEMS ARE BORN FROM THE PARENT THOUGHT OF WRONG ACTION: ALL ILLNESS, ALL DIFFICULTY, ALL SORROW, ALL TURMOIL, ALL DISAPPOINT-MENTS, ALL POVERTY.

GENERAL PRAYER TREATMENT FOR ALL PROBLEMS

The universe is founded upon the laws of perfect right action. These laws display the Mind of God and His intention toward that which He has created. I am part of that creation; therefore I am intended to profit from the law of right action.

Only my false belief can hinder the law of right action from fulfilling itself within me. Henceforth I look for the right to come forth. Whenever the wrong manifests, I shall know it to be emerging from my false belief. I shall steadfastly ignore it and place new spools carrying the thread of my new thought through the loom of Mind. I surrender myself daily to the One Perfect Right Action in all my affairs.

(Add a sentence or two of your own)_____

_____

_____

_____

Index

A

Accident-proneness, 33-34
Actuality, belief in, 101
Alcoholics Anonymous, 113, 116
Alcoholism, 62, 114-116, 118
   cure for, 121-123
   prayers for, 172
American Heart Association, 111
American Medical Association, 185
Animal kingdom, 36, 82, 157-158, 162
   disease in, 83
Anxiety (*see* Worry)
Arthritis, 33, 204-208
Asthma, 33
Atheism, 37
"Authoritative" method of treatment, 200-203

B

Babson, Roger, 5
Bacteria, 79, 82
Barrett, Elizabeth, 40
Bashfulness (*see* Shyness)
Beliefs, 29
   actuality and, 101
   experiences and, 17-19
   false, 25, 127, 167, 177, 180
   healing and, 104-105, 152-153, 210-211
   about life, 18-20, 166
   in loss, 126-130
Beloit, Wisconsin, 4, 13
Bible, the, 41, 70, 113
Body, the, and health, 110-111, 147-148
   mind and, 193-194
   (*See also* Psychosomatic medicine)